AF379325

WELL DONE

A Passionate Pursuit of Purpose

By

Shiraz Siddique

Copyright © 2023 by Shiraz Siddique

All rights reserved.

No portion of this book may be reproduced in any form without written permission from the publisher or author, except as permitted by law. For permission or bulk ordering requests, contact CBHN by email: Connect@CBHN.net

1st Edition 2023

WellDoneBook.info

Paperback: 978-1-7389648-0-2
E-Book: 978-1-7389648-1-9

In Well Done, Shiraz pierces through the layers of information overload to awaken purpose with confidence!

This book will encourage and show you how to find and then fix your eyes on your own target, keeping you in the centre of God's plan for your life.

We can easily pursue the wrong things with the right intentions. This book helps to identify and eliminate distractions by encouraging the reader to focus on the divine design inside you!

—Henoc Muamba,
Professional Athlete and
CFL Grey Cup M.O.P. 2022

Shiraz has bravely taken on the most complicated and perplexing subject a believer will face in their life: purpose. Using relatable stories, in-depth scriptural interpretation, and fundamental truths that stand the test of time, this book will compel you to become everything God made you to be with urgency like never before.

Well Done provides a framework for believers to discover or further their purpose and hurdle obstacles that are limiting their calling. Shiraz provides Bible-driven principles and actionable steps for the reader to move forward in their calling. The language is easy to understand, demystifying a lot of the Christian jargon that often leaves believers confused.

—Sathiya Sam,
Founder, DeepClean Coaching

Well Done is a strong encouragement to move forward in spite of our fears and doubts to increase our capacity to handle more of what God wants from our lives. This is a reminder that we are not limited by our resources, because God will remind us about what He can do with our five loaves and two fishes!

—Derrick Chan,
Founder, Kingdom Realty Group

Well Done reminds us that emotions can exist in tension as part of the beauty of being God's creation. In it, biblical truths are broken down in a way that's easy to understand and applicable in today's culture while still pointing back to the power of scripture.

Shiraz brings a fresh perspective and clarity to keep you moving forward in discovering or perhaps recovering your God-given purposes, in a way that's easy to understand and yet in a thought-provoking.

—Hollie Taylor,
Founder, Ten16 Entertainment and Media Host

If you desire to end your race well and hear the Lord's commendation, "Well done, good and faithful servant," then Well Done by Shiraz Siddique is for you! This book skillfully takes the reader on a journey of honest reflection of what motivates their actions and governs their resources. The book helps us to avoid pouring out our lives for a goal we thought was good, only to find that we chased the wrong one.

—Dr. Laura Lewis MD

This book explains theological doctrines in a way that is accessible. Bible stories taught in our childhood come alive again with a new meaning for adult contemporary living. The concepts are filled with imagery and axioms that will come to mind as situations arise in everyday life.

—Kevin Kirk, MTS, MBA, Senior Vice President

Well Done helps us reframe our past as preparation to harvest our future potential. It also provides a heavenly perspective on finding and living in purpose, serving as a counter-narrative to the current culture of autopilot and distracted living. You will be encouraged to live intentionally and strategically. This book is an asset that offers practical guidance on how people can release their baggage, get clarity around their purpose, and take action!

—Luiza Guimaraes

In this book, Shiraz connects with the everyday challenges we face and points us in the direction of help and reassurance. We are reminded that as long as we have breath, we also have the opportunity to head towards a brighter tomorrow.

—Delvin Edwards

In a culture that values performance and measures achievement by the approval of the masses, this book reminds us to focus on living for an audience of One.

Shiraz's style is engaging and his analogies are clear and gripping. Thank you! This is definitely a book I will read again and again. So many powerful reminders.

—Andrew Blackwood, CoachDrew.ca

Well Done connects biblical messages and God's word to earthly challenges. The author cares enough about bringing kingdom influences to the fray that he has written a book like this to reassure and strengthen us, enabling us to make better decisions.

—Bruce Wilson B.Sc., M.A.,
Director, Career Centre

This thought-provoking work blends the realities of our human experience with the principles of a full life shared in the Bible in an inspiring and encouraging way. It is a book I will read again (and again) to grasp the depth of the truth that it puts before us.

—Les Markham,
Pastor, Central Community Church

An easy to read and relatable book that speaks to any believer regardless of their age, social status, or how long they have been saved. This book speaks to the contemporary challenges that believers face when they're hit by the inevitable storms of life.

—Virginia E.

Well Done is a reminder to take high risks that defy human logic when the Lord calls us. It does not matter what others say or the endless times we fall. It spoke to my heart and gave me a boost of divine energy to pursue God's calling with a torch in one hand and a sword in the other - an excellent read!

—Athra Elias

These chapters provide the cues and clues to align our efforts with our eternal purposes. It's an invaluable guide to help us define, identify, and embrace our purpose.

—Rabih Safadi,
VP of Operations

Well Done is ideal for a group study and I look forward to doing exactly that with my LeaderImpact group! It's a blueprint for readiness when opportunity calls and also a stern reminder that if you succeed at the wrong things, you're failing already. Remember to stack your daily decisions like compound interest!

—Albert Brandstatter

Dedication

Thank you to my wife – your trust and patience has transformed me.

Thank you to my daughters – you constantly storm the norms within me.

Thank you to my family and friends – you are the force that forms me.

Above all, thank you Father God - Your grace constantly reforms me.

Acknowledgements

I want to celebrate and acknowledge the founders of
the Christian Business Harvest Network (CBHN).
It was your belief that we could inspire and uplift
a community of believers— right in the middle of
a global crisis, no less—that helped push this book
across the finish line.

It's your ongoing commitment to invest in others to
walk in the fullness of God's plans for our lives, that
keeps my resolve and resilience strong.

Albert, Lez, Sud, and Zamal, thank you for removing
the unnecessary to reveal the necessary.

Introduction

Matthew 7 and 25 sets an immensely sobering Judgment Day scene where those standing before God refer to Him as "Lord, Lord." This represents a relational connection, meaning that they were probably of His flock.

What hits between the eyes with incredible force is the Master's response: "Depart from me…" This means that Christians sitting to the left and right of us in church on a Sunday could be perishing in the pews.

Far too often, we see people living below the fullness of what God has for their lives. In most cases, it's not the lack of opportunity but a lack of faith to believe that we belong in the spaces God has mapped out for us to take dominion over.

God's grace wants to propel you into your purpose. Mercy is still crying out for us to get over our failures and get on with working towards the finish line God has set out for us. Yes, our sin should be acknowledged, but you have this book in your hand because it's time to convert your baggage into luggage.

Showing up before the Father on Judgment Day could go in one of two ways. Either you will enter into eternal rest or it's about to get extremely hot. We don't have to leave our eternal destination up to chance. It's up to us to decide if we will actively pursue and step through the open doors available to us. And when you do, your purposes will passionately activate a pursuit within you. It will happen and it will be glorious!

Table of Contents

CHAPTER ONE

Practicing Judgment Day

> Whatever is has already been, and what will be has been before; and God will call the past to account.
>
> (Ecclesiastes 3:15, NIV)

At an early age, we are encouraged to utter our first words as our parents beam with pride. These first words are usually *mama* or *dada,* followed by our ABCs and our 123s. Throughout our formal schooling, we prepare for quizzes and tests, eventually readying ourselves for high school exams. We'll then sacrifice a few more years for a college or university degree and then maybe earn an MBA or industry-specific designation.

From kindergarten to a postgraduate degree, many will spend almost twenty years learning, evaluating, and testing their knowledge and understanding to qualify for their next phases in life.

When was the last time you sat down to learn, prepare, and study for the final test, Judgment Day? Have you played out in your mind what that scene will look like? Have you thought through what you might say or how you will give an account for the resources you were provided to fulfill your purpose on the planet? Will God be like your disgruntled Grade Nine math teacher, paying close attention to see if you broke the rules? Or will His disposition be like a gracious Father gazing at you through merciful eyes?

Will the outcomes of our collective daily output provide enough fire insurance to escape eternal damnation? Is the work of the cross enough assurance, blessed assurance, to punch our tickets into eternity with Him?

Most conversations about Judgment Day revolve around elements found in Matthew 7 and 25. Tempered by the uncertainties of where we will end up in eternity, the topic of Judgment Day tends to be seen as a video replay of our lives, highlighting the good, the bad, and the ugly. We ask questions about how God will justly differentiate one's existence from the young woman who grew up in Africa, Brazil, or China. What will His criteria be? Others are wrapped up in and enraptured by the thought of seeing Him face to face and simply bowing down before Him. Does your view of Judgment Day impact how you live today?

Let's say God's design for you was to be a mechanic. However, through much deliberation and consideration, you chose to enter seminary and become a pastor—a noble choice no one would really question. Then you do good works, serve the people in your community well, and show up before God in eternity. What will the outcome of your output be?

Abraham Lincoln said it this way: "If the end brings me out all right, what is said against me won't amount to anything. If the end brings me out wrong, ten angels swearing I was right would make no difference."[1]

---

[1] Abraham Lincoln, "I do the very best I know…" *The Quotations Page*. Date of access: January 16, 2023 (http://www.quotationspage.com/quote/41305.html).

As we evaluate our lives, do we reflect His original design, or will He find us wearing fig leaves, like Adam and Eve still covering up our guilty souls? And when He comes to bless the DNA He deposited within you, will He recognize you? God will not bless your avatar!

Your blueprint was established before the foundations of the world, and you are bound to it. By building our lives according to God's specs, we avoid the shock of having it all collapse in the end. If we operate outside of His divine design, we could end up accomplishing really good things in this life but still don't pass the final test.

Our responsibility is to live a life that reflects our unshakeable belief that we are in fact made in His image, that we reflect Him. Having God recognize us and know us is key to a successful Judgment Day.

> Not everyone who says to Me, "Lord, Lord," will enter the kingdom of heaven, but only he who does the will of My Father who is in heaven. Many will say to Me on that day [when I judge them], "Lord, Lord, have we not prophesied in Your name, and driven out demons in Your name, and done many miracles in Your name?" And then I will declare to them publicly, "I never knew you; depart from Me [you are banished from My presence], you who act wickedly [disregarding My commands]."

> (Matthew 7:21– 23)

This passage provides four significant learnings:

1. Only those who do His will make the cut. Wait, what is His will for your life? (My prayer is that this book will help you receive, recover, and reinforce the path and purposes that His will has set out for you.)

2. Our works, prophesying, and casting out of demons may not be enough for us to make the cut. What looks good in church may not look good in eternity.

3. The people spoken of in the passage refer to God as "Lord, Lord," indicating that these are Christians who know who their Master is—and they still don't make the cut! This extremely sobering thought leads us to think of all the people sitting in pews beside us and in churches across the globe. If you're picturing them, are they picturing you?

4. The qualifier for eternity has little to do with what we did during our lives and everything to do with the relationship we had with Him. (*"I never knew you."*)

We will take the time to dive into the first three points in later chapters, but for now let's focus on the fourth point. This alone constitutes a critical portion of the criteria we can expect on Judgment Day.

The quantity of quality time we invest in God acts as a mirror so we can see ourselves as being made in His image. The intimate moments we initiate and prioritize with Him speak to a healthy two-way connection.

The Greek word for "knew" in Matthew 7:23 is *ginosko*[1], which has four unique yet intertwined definitions:

- "…to become acquainted with…"
- "…to know, understand, perceive…"
- "…to learn to know… to become known…"
- "…Jewish idiom for sexual intercourse between a man and a woman…"[2]

The progression in the definition of *ginosko*, from acquaintance to intimacy, represents how our relationship with God can and really should bloom. We first become aware of His presence and then get to know Him better. We begin to understand His rhythms, emotions, and movements—and these develop in us an understanding of His likes and dislikes. As we put our insights into practice, we generate greater glory from the most intimate connection we can share.

In human terms, we date, get engaged, put a ring on it, and then consummate the wedding. But relationships go beyond the wedding day and are represented in our daily action throughout marriage. Intimacy, the moments we share in private, are the hallmarks of every strong and fruitful connection.

In a message I once heard him preach, Bishop Andrew Merritt of Straight Gate Church in Detroit proposed an interesting play on the word intimacy: *into-me-you-will-see*. You will see what? We are made in His image, so naturally the more time we spend with God, the more we will become acquainted with a reflection

---

[2] "Ginosko," *Bible Study Tools*. Date of access: December 16, 2022 (www.biblestudytools.com/lexicons/greek/nas/ginosko.html).

of ourselves. So the more time we spend with Him, the more we will see who we are. This is the type of relationship that the Judgment Day scene describes: an intimate continuity of passing into eternity with Him.

It will take an overt, over-the-top investment of time and energy to build intimacy with God. How often do you make time for Him? Most of us think we are busier than we actually are. Making the time for something is very different from *having* the time. We all make time for those things we value and believe to be important.

With your eternity hanging in the balance, intimacy with God is worth it. Otherwise you could end up saying, *"Lord, Lord, I did <u>this</u> good work in your name and <u>that</u> great thing…"*. Even when we occupy ourselves with 'the hectic pace of life, He is still pursuing an intimate and deep relationship with us, one in which we can lean into His strength so He can freely pour into our lives.

In Sunday school, we are taught that at the very end of our lives we will present the sum of our works to the Father on the fateful day of judgment. All the stubble will be burned away, and what remains behind will be the gold that speaks on our behalf. We have defined gold as good works, charity, and loving thy neighbor. Or perhaps it's spending significant time in prayer and reading your Bible daily. We would all agree that these elements form the fundamental fabric of our Christian existence.

But what standard are we going to be judged against? In his book *Driven by Eternity,* noted author John Bevere writes, "You'll not be judged according to what you did, but rather according to what you were called to do!"[3]

---

[3] John Bevere, *Driven by Eternity: Making Your Life Count Today and Forever* (New York, NY: FaithWords,2006), 171.

So what is your eternal purpose? It's something you do that causes you to lose track of time. It's what keeps you up and wakes you up. It's what comes naturally to you, something which earns you greater returns for your efforts than others would be able to produce.

Take your eyes off what you aren't good at and spend more time pursuing what you sense God can make you great at! It is the pursuit and possession of our identity that qualifies us for eternity.

> It is the pursuit and possession of our identity that qualifies us for eternity.

We will spend most of our lives in between here and there, between climbing the mountaintops and digging ditches in the valleys. In other words, most of life is lived on the decline and on the incline. In this daily grind, we mine our gifts and talents to be who God has called us to be. And that's the standard against which we'll be measured. If we want to live a life that leads to being told by God, *"Well done, good and faithful servant"* (Matthew 25:21), we must grow our awareness of the calling God has created us to pursue.

As a preteen, my cousins had a pool in their backyard. Our favorite in-water game was Marco Polo. One person would be blindfolded and scream out "Marco!" No one was allowed to get out of the water, and everyone had to respond with an equally loud "Polo!" We would roam within the bounds of the pool, creating a moving target. If you were *It*, you had to rely on your ears and touch, without sight, to discern the cues and find someone to tag.

In an awkward way, that backyard pool game shaped my walk with God. It took away my sight and created a necessary dependence on my ears to hear from Him for myself and others. But instead of shouting "Marco!" and "Polo!", I cry out "Jesus!" to find my "Purpose!"

In the pool, the blindfold is the only thing blocking your view from your objective. In life, however, we all have blindfolds that block us from reaching out and laying hold of our objectives. Whether it's past failures, disappointment, underachievement, or unforgiveness, at times we all feel like a blind man following Jesus, reaching for answers that feel just out of our grasp.

It's comforting to know the answers to our questions—where to go to school, who to marry, which car to drive, and what to choose off the menu for dinner! Yet if we knew all the answers, we wouldn't need faith.

We were designed to walk by faith, depending on God for what we cannot see or comprehend. Pursuing purpose is challenging enough without adding veils that blur and warp our view. We need to stop stumbling in the dark, but it's paramount to distinguish between walking by faith and being blindfolded by guilt, blame, and shame.

In Luke 2, the rhythm and routine of life creates a U-turn that draws Jesus away from comfort towards the potency of His potential. When He hears Scripture being recited in the temple, His very DNA vibrates with excitement. The sound is so overwhelming to Him that He abandons everything in order to pursue His purpose.

Jesus's passion quite literally compelled Him to walk away from the comfort of His nest, His mother, and the rest of His clan to find the only soil that could nurture and develop the seeds of purpose within Him. This was His purpose for being on the planet. In the temple, He found Himself, reinforcing His certainty that His true identity was greater than being known as the child of Mary and Joseph.

Before Jesus wandered away from His parents in the direction of His destiny, He was simply a boy from Nazareth who was growing into a young man. Culturally, as the son of a carpenter, He would most likely have followed in Joseph's footsteps—measuring out, designing, and building stools, tables, and chairs with wood.

But imagine for a moment, what the implications would be if Jesus as a youth, built chairs that were wobbly in Joseph's shop? What if He hadn't given proper attention to the work He had been tasked with? What if He had left the place a mess and regularly missed deadlines? Would His lack of effort and indifference have discredited the work of the cross? He could have said, and perhaps you can also say, "Well, this is just temporary" or "This doesn't really matter because it's not really my purpose."

But until the fulness of time ushers you into the fulness of your purpose, everything you do right now matters. Wobbly chairs could have compromised His credibility on the cross. So evaluate and value what's in your hands right at this very moment. How you handle this season could determine your next season. What God has put in our hands are the very cues and clues that you should passionately pursue.

Becoming Better At What We Are Already Better At

In his Hall of Fame induction speech, basketball star Tim Duncan shared the famous words of St. Jerome, words that his mother had spoken into him while growing up: "Good, better, best. Never let it rest, until your good is better and your better best. They told me, and made me, to have pride in everything I did."[4]

We often hear worship songs that express honor and glory to God - your active dedication through your grind and pursuit is honoring and glorifying God. Progressing from glory to glory should be more than a cute phrase we read in 2 Corinthians 3:18. Rather, it's a command that speaks to the unleashing the DNA He deposited within us.

God's gift to us includes the skills, talents, and abilities He has baked into our blueprints. How we take the time to nurture and develop the designs written into our DNA is our gift back to the Father. Rehearsing and practicing our giftings is the greatest way to bless and glorify God. This allows us to effectively live out the first few chapters of Genesis, where God declares that everything He created is good by revealing its potential.

Becoming even better at what we're already really good at is demonstrated by how we approach our calendars, bank accounts, and effort. What opportunities do you need to invest in more so that you can glorify God?

God, the Great Evaluator, is like a proud parent waiting to see you succeed at your first piano recital. He is your greatest encourager and cheerleader. He offers grace for your mistakes and is waiting to wrap you up in His arms. Delete the thought of Him being the ultimate drill sergeant waiting for you to mess up so He can pounce at the tiniest mistake!

---

[4]Tim Duncan, "Hall of Fame Enshrinement Speech," *YouTube*. Date of access: January 16, 2023(https://www.youtube.com/watch?v=RJQTwNONd2E)

Your view of Him impacts the peace with which you develop your skills, allowing you to deliver your best when windows of opportunity open.

Isaiah 60:3 describes the moment when people of influence come to recognize your giftings as they emerge like the dawning of a new day. New days always come, so how will the world find you when the light of day shows what you were doing in the dark, working away at crafting the best version of you?

Throughout the routine of our lives, we constantly feel a nudge to step away from our nests—the comfort of security, assurance, and maybe the closest people to us—in order to pursue the greatness deposited within us. The earth groans for the full manifestation of the children of God to be revealed, and these are the children who are prepared to step into purpose and destiny.

There has never been great reward without great risk. There is no fulfillment without the type of faith God has prescribed for us. Do you want Jesus to get into your boat, or do you want to walk on water with Him?

What has God placed in your hands? For Jesus, the materials He grew up working with ultimately served His greatest purpose. Would there even have been a cross measured out, designed, and built for Him to be nailed to if He hadn't properly handled the very wood on which He bore all our sins? It may not appear that way to you, but whatever is in your hands right now is leading towards your purpose. How you handle your current assignment is a form of practice for Judgment Day.

A salesperson travelled to Minnesota and stayed in a hotel the night before his meeting with a potential client. While he slept peacefully, a massive snowstorm hit the area. In the morning, as he made his way through the lobby, he asked the bellboy if it was wise to go out into the storm. "That depends," the bellboy responded. "Do you get paid by salary or by commission?"

What mission are you on and what have you been commissioned by God to do? What is hardwired into you that will keep tugging at you until you turn and face it, chase it, and own it? Given that most of our waking hours will be spent at our nine-to-five occupations, how would others evaluate your pursuit of purpose by the effort you give on a daily basis at work? How would you evaluate your own commitment to your work?

More importantly, how will your heavenly Father consider and measure the sum of your cumulative existence? We don't have to leave this to chance. You may sense that there is still more in your core to explore. It's time to activate your blueprint and let it jump off the page into reality.

Don't fight what's in your DNA. Embrace it. Invest your time, energy, and money into it. God gifted you with your DNA, and how you discover, develop, and deliver it to the planet may be the very key to having success on Judgment Day.

Run [your race] in such a way that you may seize the prize and make it yours!

(1 Corinthians 9:24)

CHAPTER TWO

The Patch Must Match

… holding to a form of [outward] godliness (religion), although they have denied its power [for their conduct nullifies their claim of faith].

(2 Timothy 3:5)

In my childhood, Spiderman and Superman were the gold standard for superheroes. With danger rising, the web-slinging Peter Parker would don his mask to save the old lady from being robbed by menacing perpetrators! Superman could cut through metal with laser eyebeams, freeze evildoers with his frosty breath, fly around the planet in a split second, and then, without anyone noticing, slip back behind his desk at the Daily Planet!

Clark Kent's identity was safe because he knew his greatness wasn't in his cape but in his capabilities. He was Superman with or without the "S" on his chest. Likewise, whether Peter Parker was walking through the streets or swinging from building to building, his superhero identity was in his DNA.

We can distract ourselves by ensuring that we're robed in the right cape to keep up appearances. The trap is in thinking that wearing a Spiderman costume will enable us to scale the sides of skyscrapers—or that wearing the finest three-piece suit and sitting in the front row at church for Sunday service will make us better Christians.

These external trappings have the appearance of power, but unless our faith matches the mission we're on, we deny the real power we could be walking in.

Romans 8:19 says, *"Everything God made is waiting with excitement for God to show his children's glory completely"* (NCV). Which one of your identities is more real? Is it the everyday you who goes to work/school, occasionally spilling coffee on your shirt? Or is it the faith-filled, constantly praying, greater things you (John 14:12) who is assured that you have the superpower to shout down Jericho walls, restore the broken, and speak resurrection power into dry bones?

Are there days when you feel more like Clark Kent or Superman? The reality is that we're both. We should venture into deep waters for momentous moments, but eventually we all need to come back to shore. We were built to follow God's lead to walk on water, but if we don't respond in faith, we run the risk of drowning our destinies in the mushiness of mediocrity. It's difficult to live with the cape on 24/7. In the current generation, we call this "burnout," which leads us to operate at less than our optimal capacity.[5]

There is a third scenario, however, that is of greater danger than either always being Clark Kent or always trying to be Superman. It's putting on someone else's cape. It's having the appearance of godliness but lacking the power to fulfill our purpose. We can look the part, sound the part, and play the part…

---

[5] Getting burnt out reinforces the need for sabbath, which we'll discuss in greater detail in Chapter Four.

but it might end up falling apart. Or even worse, we could deny the real atomic energy stored in our DNA. We may feel like we're accomplishing good things, but not the God-ordained things He has put in our path. Then we end up walking parallel to our purpose, leaving us feeling safe but never satisfied. This is what it means to have a form of godliness but deny the power of our true DNA.

Do not incubate what God never intended you to hatch.

In Genesis 27, Jacob fools Isaac by wearing his brother Esau's "cape." Esau was more than hairy; he was so furry that it took the skin of a young goat to later recreate his appearance.

You can fool most people some of the time, but we cannot fool God at any time. But again, the real danger is fooling ourselves into chasing pursuits outside of our design, ultimately settling for less than God intended for us. Even if a kangaroo walks like a duck, quacks like a duck, and otherwise acts like a duck, he will always be a kangaroo.

But what about you? The weight of the demands and expectations of this life can hang off your neck like a strong yoke, pulling your eyes away from your true identity. In Genesis, could the yoke that Jacob wrestled to remove from his neck have been Esau's costume the whole time?

By trying to be someone other than himself, Jacob carried an ill-gotten blessing that haunted him for fourteen years. He couldn't resist the temporary progress of his trickster ways, but productivity without peace never establishes purpose. Jacob was only fooling himself and realizing this, proved to be his greatest awakening. When the sun rose after his wrestling match with God, he found that the fight had lit up his true identity. He was able to remove the cape and yoke to reveal what had been there all along: his DNA. He had to be willing to put down everything to align his ambition with his God-given mission.

> But no one puts a piece of unshrunk (new) cloth on an old garment; for the patch pulls away from the garment, and a worse tear results.
>
> (Matthew 9:16)

The process of organ donation is rigorous and meticulous for both the donor and the recipient. The donor's health needs to be at a certain level. They must be a willing participant and their blood type must be a match with the receiver. The donor must also commit to pre-op, the actual operation, and post-op recovery.

The recipient, on the other hand, knows full well how important this process is. Their body will literally reject a mismatched organ, which could result in dire consequences. To restore the recipient back to full capacity, compatibility is paramount. In other words, the patch must match.

Jesus was the perfect match to patch us up and restore us back to God's original design for us. He willingly completed His operation to provide the only blood type that was a perfect match for every person alive, so we could be in good health and prosper even as our souls prosper (3 John 1:2).

If we get the sense that something is causing us discomfort or pain, or otherwise limiting our ability to produce the type of fruit God designed us to bring forth, recognize that the perfect patch is ready. The Donor is ready. Is the recipient?

In discussing the metaphor of new wine and new wineskins (Matthew 9:14–17, Mark 2:18–22, Luke 5:33–39), the word "new" has distinct definitions. When describing new wine, the Greek word is *neos*, which means "recently revealed or what was not there before."[6] This is a recent addition to our existence, something that has not been experienced in such a way before. We have a constant desire for *neos*-new. We want a new anointing to break yokes, a new season to start afresh, and a new power to enable us to deliver more than ever before.

We tend to want to throw away the old, used elements in our lives and constantly reach for the next shiny thing, but this isn't God's only definition of new. If it was, we ourselves should have been tossed to the side a long time ago.

Thankfully, when describing new wineskins, the Greek word is *kainos*. This word means "new in quality (innovation) and fresh in development or opportunity" or "not found exactly like this before."[7] Most times we will look at something that's new as a replacement, but here we see God working on us to innovate and reveal better qualities that haven't yet been seen.

It's easier to pursue a different job, relationship, or ministry when the shine wears off. Heat, rain, dust, and movement all cause erosion and usher in the law of entropy—the gradual transition from order to disorder. Simply run your finger along the hood of your vehicle one day after a car wash and you'll see entropy at work.

---

[6] T. Oliver, "The Two Word Aspects of 'New,'" *STEM Publishing*. Date of access: January 16, 2023 (https://www.stempublishing.com/magazines/SQ/NEW2ASPC.html).

[7] "2537. kainos," *Bible Hub*. Date of access: January 16, 2023 (https://biblehub.com/greek/2537.htm).

When the new car smell fades, God is calling us to *kainos*—to refurbish, renew, and massage the hard and dry parts so we can be a better match to receive more of His power and anointing. We are the new, refurbished wineskins (*kainos*), getting ready to receive the new wine (*neos*).

We are constantly finding greater capacity, capability, and competence within ourselves—things that were not there before. As we actively allow His hands to massage out the hardened and parched areas in our lives, we can trust that He knows when we're ready to receive what He intends to pour in.

Thankfully, God isn't looking to replace us but to innovate us. Our focus should be on becoming a more pliable wineskin, trusting God with the timing. In this equation, our sole responsibility is to constantly innovate, grow, and refresh ourselves so God always finds in us a vessel to pour in fresh favor and flavor.

If the influences we keep close, the places we visit, the books we read, and the new learnings we absorb don't match up with the original purposes God gave us, we could end up living parallel to our purpose. Or worse, we could end up with more tears in our wineskins.

God is faithful, so He will *kainos* us again and again to realign us to His desired outcomes for our lives. The patch is present to restore us and renew our wineskins. Are we ready?

Stowell Theodore was a giant in my development for many years, mentoring and guiding my steps with wisdom, care, and correction. At a critical juncture in my life, I was vacillating between staying in a traditional full-time ministry role or leaving to take a senior corporate. The decision was taking a significant toll on me, so I did what I would normally do: seek counsel, and that's why I went to Pastor Stowell.

He already had an idea about what was going on. He forever changed my trajectory with these words: "The problem is that you haven't embraced the skin God gave you. Get comfortable in the skin you're in." I had wasted so many years trying to look the part and play the part which the people I respected thought was best. I thought that because I was following the popular path, I would gain credibility through association with other more recognized names.

But by leaning so hard into their thoughts, I was drowning on the guidance God was trying to provide. The truth is that I lacked the courage to claim my value and effectively devalued the goodness God had designed for me. I played a certain role, spoke a certain way, and looked a certain style in order to fit the frame others felt was best for me.

Becoming a match for the patch is all about learning to love and embrace the skin you're in. It's about embracing the tears and fears we will experience when we come face to face with reality. Applying the patch is about leaving behind that which is passed and pressing forward to what lies ahead. It's about laying hold of the plow God places in our hands to farm the fields within us to harvest the fruit He intended for us to generate. We're better off getting messy in the right soil than looking clean and missing out on eternity in a sanitized sandbox.

> We're better off getting messy in the right soil than looking clean and missing out on eternity in a sanitized sandbox.

Nor is new wine put into old wineskins [that have lost their elasticity]; otherwise the wineskins burst, and the [fermenting] wine spills and the wineskins are ruined.

> But new wine is put into fresh wineskins, so both are
> preserved.
>
> (Matthew 9:17)

The following four considerations can make us a match for the patch God is eagerly awaiting to renew our wineskins with: draining, working, stretching, and waiting.

Drain it out. God is pouring in a *neos* wine. Completely brand new. Although it's not explicitly stated, before He checks in, something needs to check out. Remnants and squatters aren't going to volunteer to leave, though, so we may need to serve—and enforce—eviction notices.

The blood of the Lamb is the greatest cleansing agent we will ever need. It can remove every stain and pain. And if God is putting a new patch on us, to repair and restore us, we need to be drained. What do you need to detox from to become a match for new wine? Admit your inability to remove the guilt and shame of sin on your own. We cannot cover ourselves up with more fig leaves, capes, and costumes. Be willing to let go of past trauma and drama. Lay it bare and become a match for new wine.

Work it out. I'm of the generation who drank soda from bottles that you could return to the store for a deposit. Cans were convenient, but they just didn't taste like the flavors that flowed from a glass bottle. The container mattered and made a difference in the experience.

In the same way, the type and quality of wineskin impacts the flavor profile of the wine as it comes into contact with the container. This means that the same anointing can sit on two different people, yet they will experience it in different ways. It's liberating to know that you can be in the Kingdom and not have to be a clone of your pastor or the other leaders around you.

The full-bodied flavor of the wine isn't complete when it's first poured into the wineskin. In fact, the type of wine you pour into a wineskin is known as young wine. Young wine interacts with the wineskin to patiently mature and develop its flavors. The symbiotic relationship between the wine and wineskin produces a unique savor, almost as unique as one's fingerprint.

For young wine to mature and develop its robust taste, it is the responsibility of both the wine and wineskin. The vinedresser can choose to pour the liquid into any container, but he needs to be aware of the relationship between wine and skin. The right wine needs to be matched with the right wineskin.

A farmer will prepare the soil before the seed is planted, so why would we expect God to pour a new anointing, enablement, and empowerment into us if we aren't ready? God's timing preserves and propagates the potential of both the wine and the wineskin. So while you're waiting on God, ensure that you're working to develop the skin you're in. Remember, we carry the responsibility to get even better at what we're already better at.

Stretch it out. A number of years ago, I spoke at a young adult retreat that had a spa onsite. The conference hosts encouraged me to experience the best massage the area had to offer. Back then, a massage wouldn't have been in even my top-fifty activities, but at their recommendation I decided to give it a try.

When I arrived for my massage, I informed the masseur that this was a whole new experience for me. He could tell I was hesitant and calmly explained, "Once you remove all your layers of clothing, I can get in there to stretch you out."

After all the pushing and pulling, which felt painful in the moment, I felt taller walking out of that place.

We become more pliable and elastic as we learn new things. Becoming more elastic means stretching outside of our comfort zone to reach the fruit on the highest branches. We hear about striving for new goals, but remember what God has said: *"What no eye has seen, nor ear heard, nor the heart of man imagined, what God has prepared for those who love him"* (1 Corinthians 2:9, ESV). So the next time you state your goals and objectives, stretch them and watch God as He follows through.

It's not always easy. For example, when it came to my massage:

- I had to make the time and then keep the appointment.
- I had to remove all my layers of clothing so the masseur could work deep into the tissue to reach the issues causing tension and tightness.
- It did not feel relaxing. As matter of fact, it was painful.
- I had to trust the process.

God wants to get His hands on you, but will you remove the outer layers? You will feel vulnerable and exposed, but can you trust the process enough to let it stretch you out? The only way He can work out the kinks of your wineskin is if you let Him in—and this will only happen when you make the time and keep your appointments with Him.

Perhaps we aren't as pliable in His hands as we once were, but that's His area of expertise. He's still massaging out our mistakes and heartaches. A dormant wineskin can be reactivated with His touch. God doesn't waste a thing.

Unless you renew and grow, there's no room for the wine to flow!

What was the last significant learning experience you went through? What was the last challenge you struggled with? Spiritual calisthenics create room for the wine to flow!

Consistently stretching keeps the arthritis out of our souls and allows us to keep pressing towards the high calling He has set before us.

Wait it out. I've heard too many stories about people who aborted the mission they were on because they couldn't last beyond the point of inflection to get to the other side of their journey. A few of those stories are my own!

Our paths will always be littered with exit ramps and we'll have every excuse to pull off. How long does a good wine take to develop the robust flavors it needs in order to be considered world-class? The reality is that quality always takes a certain quantity of time, and whoever lasts the longest wins. If you can outlast the last piece of cheesecake that's calling your name in the fridge, you win. If you can walk past those pairs of shoes calling your name while living on a budget, you win. If you don't give up until you possess the promises you sense God has for you, you win.

Pressing the fast-forward button is like eating raw chicken. Nobody wins. Taking premature actions means you still have an immature mindset. You need to decide if the long game is worth it. You need to decide if *you* are worth the wait.

A study conducted in the 1940s by Nikolaas Tinbergen and Konrad Lorenz focused on the rolling behavior of the greylag geese. The researchers noted,

The sight of the displaced egg triggers this mechanism. If the egg is taken away, the animal continues with the behavior, pulling its head back as if an imaginary egg is still being maneuvered by the underside of its beak. However, it will also attempt to move other egg shaped objects, such as a golf ball, door knob, or even an egg too large to have possibly been laid by the goose itself.[8]

Instinctively, greylag geese, as well as other birds, will pull round objects that look like eggs towards their nest. The appearance of the object attracts the goose and compels them to treat it like their own egg.

In 2 Timothy 3:5, we read about the same danger—of simply being in the presence of forms of godliness, not the fullness. The message is strong, encouraging us to have nothing to do with the type of people who have a certain appearance but no substance. In effect, they deny the fullness of the power in which they could actually operate.

We aren't asked to pursue everything that looks good. Are you certain that the thoughts you meditate on are worth manifesting in your life? Don't nurse and incubate that which God never intended for you to hatch! Lookalikes can lead to forms of godliness, wasting our time; they will never equal the harvest God intended for you to birth.

On a shopping trip with my then teenage daughters, I overheard a conversation between two young women. One asked the

---

[8] "Fixed Action Pattern," *Bionity.com*. Date of access: January 16, 2023 (https://www.bionity.com/en/encyclopedia/Fixed_action_pattern.html).

other, "Do these jeans make me look thin?" Her friend responded, "Well maybe try these on…"

In contrast, a number of years ago, my wife and I went to New York City to see our dear friend Chantel Riley perform at her opening night on Broadway. She is an immensely talented actress who needs to stay fit for the strenuous dancing components of her show.

We went to dinner with her afterward, and the entire time I noticed that the guys walking by stared a little longer at her than they should have. Extremely annoyed by the unwanted attention, she finally blurted out, "I'm just sitting here in my sweats and they still won't leave me alone!"

My wife chimed in. "Hey, when you're fit, it doesn't matter what you're wearing on the outside!"

Focus less on what makes you look good and more on what it takes to *be* good. Focus less on keeping up appearances and more on what it takes for God to recognize you as His own. That's the difference between having a form of godliness or the fullness of what God really has for you. There is no power in the superhero costume. The power is in the one who wears it. Focus on your wineskin and be a better match for the patch; your eternity might be on the line.

CHAPTER THREE

The Rich Get Richer. Amen!

If you do well [believing Me and doing what is acceptable and pleasing to Me], will you not be accepted? And if you do not do well [but ignore My instruction], sin crouches at your door; its desire is for you [to overpower you], but you must master it.

(Genesis 4:7)

In **Matthew 25,** we read three parables that share a common thread that reinforce one another. The first parable is about the ten virgins; five were prepared while the others were not. Next, we come to the parable of the talents, in which two out of three workers worked with the resources they were given to grow their results. Finally, we encounter a Judgment Day scene, where God separates those with an appearance of godliness from those whom He recognizes as His own.

All three parables bifurcate the haves and the have-nots. All three have the same intertwined theme: what you do when no one's watching matters.

But while they were going away to buy oil, the bridegroom came, and those who were ready went in with him to the wedding feast; and the door was shut and locked. Later the others also came, and said, "Lord, Lord, open [the door] for us." But He replied, "I assure you and most solemnly say to you, I do not know you [we have no relationship]."

(Matthew 25:10–12)

Matthew 25 begins with the parable of the ten virgins, all of them ripe with anticipation for the arrival of their groom. The New Testament includes a few analogies in which Jesus is represented as a groom and the Church is His bride.

In this parable, the ten virgins represent the many who make up the Church. They have been taught what to do at the wedding, but they don't all prioritize their preparation for the groom's arrival. They all really want to meet the groom, but for many of them it won't have a happy ending.

All ten virgins fall asleep full of anticipation, but they wake up to different realities. They hear shouts of "He's coming! Go out to meet him!" The ones who prepared themselves ahead of time by bringing enough oil for their lamps are now able to make their way to the groom.

However, those who didn't prepare—who didn't align their actions with their intentions—end up missing out right at the finish line.

Like the ten virgins, the way in which we prepare and take accountability for our time and effort will have a direct impact on the realities we live in. How we spend our present moments will either lighten the load or add to the weight we have to lift every morning.

In Canada, we see clear evidence as one season shifts into another. When fall turns to winter, both the temperature and the leaves begin to drop. This ushers in the official start of sweater season.

We all know the first snowfall is coming, yet so many Canadians fail to make the necessary adjustments. For example, when the roads first get icy, there's a spike in car accidents every year. These people didn't ready themselves for the change that was inevitable. Likewise, all ten virgins knew the groom was coming but only half were ready. If you were to evaluate your preparedness for your next season, would you be ready?

What signs are you tracking in order to recognize the coming change? What do you look for as your purposes ripen? It's not about pinning down the precise moment when the change happens; it's about training our eyes to recognize the signs.

In the parable, all ten virgins were so close to the finish line, but half the group missed out by messing up their preparation. Your next season is always on the horizon, so how are you preparing?

I'm empathetic towards the five who ran out of oil, as well as the prodigal son who tried to forge his own identity. I also empathize with the guy with only one talent, from the parable that begins in Matthew 25:14. He only had one talent of gold, and to make matters worse that one talent got taken away and given to the guy who already had plenty.

Although it hardly seems fair, God gave a directive to take from the poor and give to the rich. It only appears unfair until we look into the mindset of the one-talent guy.

> So I was afraid [to lose the talent], and I went and hid your talent in the ground. See, you have what is your own.
>
> (Matthew 25:25)

This man's fear of failure was greater than his excitement for potential success. So he played it safe and avoided risk. Interestingly, he wasn't actually lazy. He did in fact take action. He spent time planning and followed through by finding a place to dig a hole, bury his bag, and cover it up again. God called him lazy because he applied effort towards taking the easy way out. Shortcuts always seem to short-circuit the potency of our purpose.

Given my soft spot for the one-talent guy, I pursued understanding and heard God speak softly to my spirit: *"The rich get richer..."* In my cynicism, my inner response was, "Yeah. I hate that it works that way. That's not right." But every time I read this passage, I kept sensing God adding an amen: *"The rich get richer. Amen."*

Why would God stamp and validate that statement?

God was pointing out the real problem: me. I saw myself as the poor getting poorer, not as the highly favored of God growing in blessings. I was handcuffed to a victim mentality that felt that the system was working against me. I read that all things work together for my good and boisterously sang songs of moving from glory to glory, but did I believe that could be for me?

No. I had faith that all things were possible, but maybe not for me. Because I was afraid, I barricaded my bags of gold behind every excuse to justify and explain why I couldn't succeed. Then it was easy to fail.

At a certain point in my life, I would have been happy to break even and simply return to God what He had given me. Until I realized that the math of breaking even equals eternal damnation.

For whoever has [spiritual wisdom because he is receptive to God's word], to him more will be given, and he will be richly and abundantly supplied; but whoever does not have [spiritual wisdom because he has devalued God's word], even what he has will be taken away from him.

(Matthew 13:12)

It took some time for me to shift from overvaluing opinions, commentary, and crowd noise to recognize that God sees His children as the rich getting richer. Being "rich" is more than a financial measure. It includes being rich in wisdom. It includes having an abundance of energy and enlarging our capacity to maximize time. Being rich means developing solid, mutually beneficial relationships. It's about our cups flowing over so God can pour into us that which we didn't even know we sowed.

The Beauty of the Cross: there is no loss. He redeems it all.

To address the sabotaging thoughts embedded in us, we need to renew our minds. We think to ourselves, *I deserve...* and *That's not fair...* Holding on to injustice only poisons our own potential. Remember that a loving Father sacrificed His only begotten Son, who truly didn't deserve the atrocities of the cross. Using that scale to balance our concept of fair helps us get past the drama and trauma of what happens around us.

On the flipside, we could be drawn to equally limiting thoughts like, *We don't deserve this.* And we would be right; we *don't* deserve what we've been given. That's the beauty of the cross. Maintaining an understanding of our deservingness looks like humility, gratitude, and a determination to give our best effort. We must not take His sacrifice for granted.

With focused attention, His intentional grace can rejuvenate our outlook. We could tell God about our limited resources, but He might remind us about what He can do with our five loaves and two fishes. Instead of feeling like we don't have enough time, we can shift to maximizing the time we do have. Instead of feeling lethargic, we can eat healthier and exercise. Rewiring ourselves in these ways will limit us from taking orders from our temporary emotions and keep our eternal picture in mind. Renewing our minds reinforces that we do have enough— because He is more than enough!

> If you do well [believing Me and doing what is acceptable and pleasing to Me], will you not be accepted? And if you do not do well [but ignore My instruction], sin crouches at your door; its desire is for you [to overpower you], but you must master it.
>
> (Genesis 4:7)

Like the one-talent guy, Cain was bitter because of a perceived injustice. Instead of heeding God's warning and guidance, Cain went to his brother Abel to complain and ultimately lost the battle with his anger.

The warning here is strong: do well with what you have while you have it. If you don't, the wages of sin and will rule over you for eternity. Cain did the least but expected the most. Abel did the most and trusted God to be faithful and just.

> To one he gave five bags of gold, to another two bags, and to another one bag, each according to his ability. Then he went on his journey.
>
> (Matthew 25:15, NIV)

In Acts 10:34, we read that God is not a respecter of persons, meaning that he wasn't playing favorites when He gave out units of five talents, two talents, and one talent in the parable in Matthew 25. In fact, if these investments are measured by percentage, then the two-talent guy and the five-talent guy received the exact same doubling effect.

There are three gifts represented in this parable, and the rich get richer because they understand the first gift: we are already inherently rich in potential. The word ability in Matthew 25:15, in Greek, is *dynamin*, which means "a specially activated force."[9] The five-talent guy had already activated a greater force, having mined his ability before God even opened the doors of opportunity.

We tend to focus on the second gift, which is the reward of five turning into ten. But the recognition and development of the first gift is a powerful multiplying force that will see your trees fill with fruit.

From athletes to actors, these days we hear everyone quote 1 Corinthians 10:13, the assurance that God will not give us more than we can handle. This scripture is interpreted in terms of handling hardship but discovering and developing what's in your DNA is hard work! In context, this passage is actually about temptation. The daily temptation to drift from the direction of our DNA is strong. Staying the course is that *dynamin* force that leads to daily developing our DNA when no one sees or seems to care.

In Matthew 25:15, God uses the exact same principle: He doesn't give the three men in the parable more than they can

---

[9] "δύναμις," *Bill Mounce*. Date of access: January 16, 2023 (https://www.billmounce.com/greek-dictionary/dynamis).

handle. He gives each according to how they managed to develop their abilities. He gives each exactly what they had already demonstrated the capacity to handle.

> The rich (you) get richer when you increase your capacity to handle what has already been gifted to you in your DNA.

The rich (you) get richer when you increase your capacity to handle what has already been gifted to you in your DNA.

There is still a third, rather unexpected gift available. The five-talent guy received the bag of gold from the one-talent guy because he had a passion to activate and continually sharpen his skills. This constant pursuit of growth in wisdom and stature leads to more favor with God and favor with man (Luke 2:52).

What was the last real learning process you committed to that developed in you greater critical thinking, rewired your habits, and built your stamina to last longer and go farther? When we don't manage our resources well, God will simply hand them over to someone else who will.

I've spent more time than I'd like to admit with pastors who have a heart for ministry but refuse to develop in these ways. Leaders who develop themselves are shepherds whom God can trust with more sheep. God will release people from one-talent organizations, churches, or businesses and they will head over to the five-talent guy. This migration will be God's doing.

Some might interpret this as being unfair, but when have we ever heard that life will be fair on this side of the grave? The takeaway is to be fair to the richness of the DNA within you and begin to see yourself as the rich getter richer. You are worth it, and it is written in the blueprints of your design.

If you grew up watching *Sesame Street*, you may be familiar with the segment called "One of These Things." Four items are displayed, three of which are similar while the other is different. The object is to identify the item that doesn't belong.

In Matthew 25, God zooms in His lens to pursue a similar exercise. He evaluates similar items, and some may not make the cut.

For example, from a distance sheep and goats may appear similar. But once you get a little closer, you'll see the differences. How close are you with God? The more time you spend with one another, the assurance of being identified as His own will grow.

In Luke 10, we find the parable of the good Samaritan. A man is beaten by robbers and left on the side of the road. A few people pass by the beaten man, but then a Samaritan stops to attend to his needs.

The Samaritan people were relatives of the Israelites but were shunned by them.

Thankfully, however, God looks at what's inside and not the titles or stereotypes others try to attach to us.

The helpful man became known as the good Samaritan because his heart and actions lovingly aligned to serve his neighbor. The good Samaritan didn't justify his compassion towards the beaten man based on his credentials or worthiness. It was not the Samaritan's pedigree, appearance, or long, drawn-out prayers that qualified him to be God's appointed servant of the hour; it was the purity of his service.

If you need to know exactly where God is so you can tend to Him, you might walk right past the opportunity. Finding your next move of God may be as simple as moving outside your front door and looking to the left and right.

The rich get richer when we recognize opportunities to be God's hand extended to the ones who need His love most. In His sermon on the mount, Jesus says, *"Blessed are those who mourn"* (Matthew 5:4). Why? Because we are going to show up to support them! And we are encouraged to give to the needy without needing to be seen doing it (Matthew 6:2). Trust that God sees and is faithful and just to recognize us. Be His sheep and then be the type of sheep whose actions attract God's attention and favor.

A silent God does not equal a missing God.

Most of us have questioned or cried out, "God, where are You?" We hear this from the ten virgins wondering what the delay could be to the goats who said, "God, did You not see?" Where was God when a loved one was ill? Many of us just need direction, wanting to know His will.

The three parables of Matthew 25 present us with the posture we need to maintain while the master observes from a distance. During school exams, the examiner is always present in the room but remains silent. Leading up to the final exams, we as students controlled our calendars. We controlled our effort and the amount of distraction we gave in to. The degree to which we held ourselves accountable determined how committed we were to mastering the test.

A mentor of mine for many years, frequently said, "When the student is ready, the master will appear." Get prepared. Measure your actions. Be accountable. The master is coming to deliver five talents or two talents or one talent. What will you receive? God's silence doesn't mean He has gone away. A quiet God never means an absent God.

To prepare simply means to make ready—beforehand. This word represents our ability to move forward without seeing. Noah believed that God had instructed him to construct the largest vessel of his day. He believed, so he prepared and acted.

Before Noah could begin, though, God provided the blueprint for him to build the Ark (Genesis 6:14–22). In Moses's case, he was the vessel being prepared in Pharoah's house to lead the largest people movement of the day (Exodus 2:10).

We hear people say, "When will my turn come?" The truth is that everyone will have their day, but will you be ready when yours comes?

Esther was asked by her uncle if she had been put in the position of queen for such a time as this (Esther 4:14). God prepared a whale for Jonah, a slingshot for David, a husband for Mary, and a whole planet for Adam and Eve!

The ten virgins received intel on the groom's arrival but only five of them prepared properly. Preparation is the evidence and substance of God-pleasing faith. So how are you preparing? Surely the resources you require have already been made ready— before you stepped into your season.

Everyone seems to be searching for a word from God—but when He speaks, then what? Following through is the practical side of prophecy. Faith means moving forward even if we don't yet see the evidence.

A farmer plants seed in the spring because he trusts the process. Who knows if there will be a drought or if a vicious storm may rip through? The farmer still puts in the dirty work that others will never fully appreciate.

In the same way, faith doesn't guarantee us our exact desired outcome, but we will never know what the possibilities are unless we take action. A specific action may not work… but what if it does? It's wise to be more afraid of missing out than messing up. God can deal with your messes, but missing out might have eternal implications.

Our actions will speak louder than any words spoken in your favor, or even words that are meant to slander us. Intermittently, we all come up against voices that question or oppose the path we feel God prompting us to pursue. These voices will want us to justify our actions. They will want us to be "reasonable." But a reliable God would never ask us to venture down a path that's unreliable. So ultimately the actions we take should impact only one Voice—and that's the one with the power to declare either "Depart from me" or "Well done."

Adam had a pivotal conversation with God in which he tried to shift the blame for his actions by pointing the finger at his wife. Like the one-talent guy, Adam found a way to explain away his actions and put the accountability at the feet of someone else. This type of justification seems to come naturally to us. And yet Matthew 25 shows us that God places great weight on us taking responsibility for our own resource management.

What great thing would you do if you knew you couldn't fail? Perhaps this is a better question: what great thing would you continue to work harder at even if your efforts appear to hardly work? But you continue to get up and grind because something in your spirit unshakably tells you to press on.

In all three parables, the Master is away—but He soon returns to see how accountable the people were with their time, energy, and finances. All three call on us to make preparations before our season begins. We are to be accountable to how we will spend eternity.

The one-talent guy succumbed to the notion that God was unjust and unreasonable. The irony is that he was right; we should all be unreasonable as well. Literally, be un*reason*able. Lose the ability to require rationale before taking an action. Just go when you get a sense that God has said so. His ways aren't like our ways, so how can we expect to fully understand all the hows and whys?

Despite our folly and failure, God's commitment to us is unreasonable. If we were running the show, we would have dropped ourselves a long time ago, considering all the egregious ways in which we have let down the Father. Yet He has not walked away from us. Rather, He celebrates our achievements.

Would you still give God the benefit of the doubt in any area of your life, even if there was no reasonable possibility of success? Trusting in God is the key to believing that His plans for us will generate a brighter future. Our actions require only one litmus test: God said so, so we go.

Faith isn't a guarantee that our desired outcomes will immediately bear fruit, but we demonstrate our faith by getting back up even if we fall because we believe that inherent in every setback is a new way to attack the challenge. Keeping our faith fruitful requires relinquishing control and learning to lean into His reliability.

Following God's prompt without a justifiable reason is the type of faith that pursues purpose even if others say "Noah, that boat has no reasonable chance to float" or "Jonah, those Ninevites don't even deserve your time or effort" or "Mary, Joseph has no reason to marry a pregnant woman!" If God had to set things on fire to make it plain to Moses, there will be signs and guideposts for you as well! The giants of our faith had to be unreasonable in their risk- taking, faith-developing, glory-to-glory pursuit. Such pursuits led them to uncover, discover, and recover their passion and purpose.

As your faith becomes more faithful, and your grace grows more graceful, trust that He is moving you from glory to glory, from rich to richer. Amen.

CHAPTER FOUR

On that Day Two Grind

In this you rejoice, though now for a little while, if necessary, you have been grieved by various trials, so that the tested genuineness of your faith—more precious than gold that perishes though it is tested by fire—may be found to result in praise and glory and honor at the revelation of Jesus Christ.

(1 Peter 1:6–7, ESV)

Christmas lovers have a strong argument. But for me, Easter is the season I look forward to most. What could be more amazing than celebrating Jesus kicking death in the teeth, ripping away the keys of life and death, and re-establishing a direct connection to the Father?

We revere day one of the Easter weekend as Good Friday, when on that cross He bore all our sin and shame. Then there is also day three: Easter Sunday, baby! We celebrate the all-time greatest Champion who rises again, robs the grave, and asks, "Where oh grave is your victory?"

Easter is about tragedy then triumph, devastation then deliverance. It's definitely my favorite time of the year!

We call it Easter weekend, but do you know anyone who celebrates Saturday? Day two is like the forgotten middle child as we endure twenty-four seemingly meaningless hours to arrive at the big day. I don't know what you do on that day… I don't even know what I do… but we should intentionally consider what we were meant to do. There is no day three without day two. There is no resurrection power unless we endure our darkest hour. There is no throne room without the tomb.

The Bible doesn't explicitly detail Jesus's exploits between the cross and resurrection, but we can agree that it was more than catching up on sleep. We do know that while the disciples were frantically calculating and calibrating their next moves, Jesus was completing the redemptive work of the cross when no one could see, grinding away in the dark. He was calmly securing the keys of life and death so we too could be raised to life in Him.

Like the disciples, our hope in a brighter future can fade in the face of tragedy and disappointment. We can be left to wonder whether our lives can be better than what we're currently experiencing. It can feel like we're marching inside a hamster wheel, going nowhere. We must decide whether our purposes are still worth pursuing. Is it worth it? Are *we* worth it?

Day two is about endurance, perseverance, and embracing the grace for your race. If things are looking bleak and you feel weak, know that resurrection is coming. Reinforcements are on the way. How can we be sure? Because Easter Sunday always comes! Handle your day two well.

Regardless of culture or geography, a great glass of wine remains a part of the joy and pain of the human experience. Consider, however, the crushing that a grape endures in order for us to extract its sweet nectar. Now that's pressure! Equally potent in the pain of producing a great vintage is the patience required to produce a refined wine.

You can tell how much someone wants something by the amount of pain and patience they are willing to endure to obtain it. The fermenting process is a chemical reaction between the yeast (the Kingdom of God) and the sugars (our sweet spot), resulting in a reaction that leads to transformation. We generally reside in one of the following three stages of fermentation.

Stage #1: Young wine. We're full of potential, but in this instant gratification, drive-thru age, we have a tendency to get jumpy and move before God tells us. It's like pulling seed out of the ground to see for yourself whether the plant has sprouted. Such people walk by sight, not by faith.

Patience is a virtue. It preserves and protects your harvest from adolescent exuberance. Maturity regulates anticipation, ensuring that we don't cash out early and miss out on the fullness of the flavors He is developing within us. Fermentation is the process of waiting in the darkness of the wineskin for the potency of our purpose to develop.

Stage #2: Overfermentation. It's equally wasteful and dangerous to lag behind as it is to impatiently sprint ahead of God. Missing out because of your own insecurities demonstrates a lack of faith that God will do what He said He will.

A business mentor of mine bakes ambiguities into any new endeavor he launches. He believes that you can build a plan sixty percent of the way to completion, but you will never know the remaining forty percent without activating and acting on that plan.

Allowing past negative experiences to influence our future moves keeps us on the sidelines watching God pour His goodness into others instead of us.

The chemical result of overfermentation transforms wine into vinegar, releasing gases that can knock you out and others around you. Missing opportunities is marked by bitterness, the pain of regret, and perhaps even shame. Avoid expiry dates by taking your shots when you have them. Is this your time?

Stage #3: Ripe and ready. Luck has been defined this way: opportunity meeting preparedness. Such a definition creates shared accountability. God controls the timing while we absolutely hold the responsibility to prepare.

It's not about you alone; this world waits in earnest anticipation for you to be revealed. And yet how well you ferment will cement your value when you're on full display. God will open windows of opportunities, but will you be ready? That encapsulates the day two grind: patiently preparing for the potency of your potential to be poured out.

In the book of Judges, Samson's feats and failures are on full display as he wrestles with the purposes he was groomed to fulfill. Set apart with a Nazarite vow with the clear mandate to lead Israel as a judge, Samson should have developed great focus and stature. But somewhere along the way, his character resisted the restraint required in his proverbial day two.

Given his wayward lifestyle, filled with overindulging on wine, women, and violence, it's entirely fair to deliver a negative postmortem of his life. But Samson's challenge was more than his inability to maintain his righteousness; he didn't respect and wasn't accountable for his purpose—and ultimately his Judgment Day.

Before we zoom in further, though, let's recognize that all our best works amount to filthy rags (Isaiah 64:6). We too fall short. The day two grind amplifies the role that character plays in getting us to the other side when we're in between here and there. Our character will either erode or contribute to our calling. It will propel or poison our purpose.

In Romans 7, the apostle Paul said that he had failed to do what He should and often did what he never intended. The struggle is real for all of us. The day two grind is about responding well to mistakes, mishaps, and momentary lapses in judgment. Having good character doesn't mean that we avoid failure; it means that we accept that we'll fall short. But because we believe, we repeatedly rise and keeping grinding until His glory shines through. How well we respond to failure is infinitely more crucial than our fall.

In Judges 16, Samson was literally on the grind, crushing the Philistine's wheat under a giant millstone. Meant to be a righteous judge for the Israelites, the lure of loose living had fractured his focus. His desire for Delilah, and her entrapment, had blinded him. He had lost his vision long before His eyes were brutally cut out of their sockets.

What we focus on grows to the point that it consumes our view, acting like cataracts, blurring the clarity of our calling.

And now Samson was going in circles, grinding grain in a Philistine prison. That grind, however, served to renew his strength. It delivered his greatest victory over the sworn enemies of his soul. The Great Redeemer never wastes an opportunity to glorify our grind and turn defeat into deliverance.

In John 11, a crowd gathered as Jesus approached the tomb of his close friend Lazarus. A major obstacle stood in the way of Mary and Martha being able to hold their brother alive again; he had died. But his sisters believed Jesus could have saved him if only He had arrived before the clock struck midnight on their faith.

We often speak hopeless commentary like "It's too late..." or "It's not possible..." in a feeble attempt to saddle the Creator of the universe with our own limitations. We place the onus for breakthroughs at the feet of Jesus, depending on Him to snap a better reality into existence with His fingers.

In John 11, however, Jesus places the responsibility squarely where it belongs:

> Jesus said, "Take away the stone." Martha, the sister of the dead man, said to Him, "Lord, by this time there will be an offensive odor, for he has been dead four days! [It is hopeless!]"
>
> (John 11:39)

Jesus doesn't move the stone. In fact, He instructs Mary and Martha to move it. Are we waiting on God or is He waiting on us? Whether it's a tombstone, a millstone, or the fear of the unknown, He is calling more than Lazarus to come forth; He is calling your faith to resurrection and your dry bones to come to life.

The directive to move stones is about birthing within us a bold belief to reach beyond the tomb. That type of faith rises to God as a sweet and pleasing aroma.

What was more of an offensive odor to God, Lazarus's rotting corpse or Martha's lack of faith? Undoubtedly the stench of Lazarus was strong but consider the stale odor that rises from stalled or dying dreams.

The beauty of the cross is that there's no loss. He corrects us and resurrects us. He turns our mourning into dancing and our sorrow into joy. If you're experiencing a dormant, delayed, or derailed dream, Jesus can speak a better word and declare, "Come forth."

But we play a role in how we emerge from an emergency, so begin to pray for and seek ways to move past indecision and into activation. The reason you feel buried might not be your fault—and yes, people can be responsible for your pain—but you are responsible for partnering with God for your prosperity. Reach for the closest stone and push.

Picture God directly pouring down ideas, connections, and open doors through a dedicated conduit that leads right to us. Our ability to receive is based on the clutter, noise, and negative thoughts in that exclusive pipeline, all of which pollute the purity of His guidance. It's like watering a beautiful garden with a bent and leaky hose. Our response might be to blast the nozzle to increase the flow of God in our lives, but that leads to more leakage. Why would God pour out more if we can't handle and hold on to what we already have? It's crucial to consistently clean out our conduits, patch up the leaks, and find the bend in the hose.

Fixing the flow of His requires us to recharge our batteries.

My wife and I invested in electric bikes to better our health and to explore new places. One summer ride we took was a fifty-kilometer round trip through the Blue Mountain region of Ontario towards a quaint waterside town called Thornbury.

The return was going to be mostly uphill, so our strategy was to manually pedal on the way there to preserve our battery power boost for moments of weariness on the way back.

Our start was delayed by more than an hour, but we got past it. The temperature was cooler than we had expected, but we overcame that too. It soon began to rain, making for a slippery trail, but determination steadied our focus.

About ninety minutes into our trip, my battery dipped to twenty-five percent. We made the difficult decision to turn back… all because I had failed to charge my battery the night before. As usual, my wife was gracious even after later discovering that we had been mere minutes away from our destination!

For us, day one included an idea and a plan to ride to Thornbury. Day two presented multiple excuses to bail on our day one plans, but we pressed ahead. Day three never arrived, because we (meaning me) didn't prepare properly.

Jesus told us to consider the cost before you start building a house, lest you find yourself with an incomplete structure. Outlasting leaner times to celebrate more finish lines absolutely requires us to clean out our conduits, straighten the bend in the hose, and keep our batteries charged. The following considerations will help you power through more day twos.

Worship. Demonstrating gratitude and refocusing on the grandeur of who He is reminds us that the God of the universe is for us and on our side. He inhabits the very praises of His people, creating an atmosphere of possibilities. When a good Father shows up, he always has gifts and surprises in tow. Worship is like a giant reset button that refreshingly reminds us that He is our partner in life.

Sleep. The best mornings begin with even better nights. The neuro-scientific evidence of brain rejuvenation through sleep is astounding. This isn't about becoming a morning person; it's about recharging properly regardless of when you start your day. Your daily IV drip of caffeine provides temporary focus but can't slow your heartbeat, relax your muscles, or invite ideation through imagination of His still small voice. Sleep reduces stress-inducing cortisol levels, repairs cell tissue, and allows your mind to process the previous day's intake without distraction. Yes, sleep is that beneficial!

Sabbath. Many people feel like they don't have enough time to mark the sabbath. However, the sabbath isn't about having time but loving the discipline of making and taking the time away from our nine-to-five activities to reset, refuel, and relaunch. It flushes out the negatives in our lives because we choose to meditate on the positive.

If God Himself took time off when creating the earth, regimenting downtime should take on a whole new meaning for us. Prioritizing our relationships with God, family, and friends is an important element of sabbath and keeps the main building blocks of our lives in clear view. The concept of burnout is huge and a regimented sabbath is the antidote.

God understands the stress tests of our design, so He modelled what it takes to pull back from the brink of an empty tank in order that we not find ourselves at the side of the road out of gas. Taking a break to check our gauges allows us to reflect and course-correct, ensuring that the path we're on ends in a fruitful outcome.

At the very least, consider the sheer enormity of data our minds are exposed to on a daily basis. The chaos this creates is immense, so begin the day with sabbath for the brain—a conscious reprieve from the flurry of activity that can overwhelm us.

Sabbath is like rebooting our operating system before it hangs or freezes. If you aren't operating as efficiently or optimally as you believe you should, hit the restart/sabbath button and repeat regularly. This will regulate your performance, patience, and power to overcome the challenges that constantly curtail your ability to rise above a mediocre existence!

Alone time. Jesus constantly retreated on His own so that He could later return with supernatural power. Joseph set aside all his possessions and closest relationships, then crossed over a river to wrestle through his past alone with God, gaining freedom in the present and ultimately his eternal future. Moses stood alone on a mountaintop with God, and Elijah met Him in the cleft of a rock.

The intrusive access we have granted technology leads to us being bombarded with more than two thousand messages on a daily basis. I'm not a technology hater, but we should monitor any area of our lives that has free and untethered access to our attention. All these messages make it nearly impossible to be alone, blessed with a blank slate in our thoughts.

It's not about being alone, though, but being alone with God. Daniel was alone in a lion's den, but he too was not alone. Jonah was inside a whale's intestines and wasn't alone, proving that we are never truly alone. Psalm 139:8 tells us that even if we make our bed in hell, God is there.

The question is, once you're alone, how long does it take to sift through your thoughts to be alone with God? Quieting our minds is a deliberate discipline that allows the Great Chiropractor to reset us and ensure that every movement works for us and not against us. His voice can pierce through the noise.

Community. It is good and pleasing to gather together in unity, but the point here is to guard who you gather with. Consider how you feel after being in someone's presence. Do they act like a shot of adrenaline, leaving you to feel motivated enough to move mountains, or are you left feeling depleted and low on energy? With each of the people in your life, hit save or delete. We need to intentionally determine how close we keep with those we consider friends, even if it's family.

Technology. Jesus is still answering prayers to make our burdens lighter, which is why I firmly believe He sent us the great minds in our day and age who have created productivity apps. Adopting technologies that reduce the strain on our time, energy, and financial resources also makes our yoke easier. Accounting, booking trips, ordering meals, and tracking the daily steps we take are all made simple by using productivity apps. The mission never changes, but the methods absolutely do!

Health. We can fix the flow of His favor in our lives by continually investing in and developing our health. The food we eat, our exercise regiment, and the time we take to focus on ourselves will build and maintain two of our greatest God-given assets: our body and mind.

On the one hand, we can pray for more energy or we can purchase a gym membership, new running shoes, and a step tracker. There is no question that eating healthier makes the wallet lighter, but you need to decide whether you're worth it. Is the quality of life you desire worth it? Are your eternal purposes worth it? Consider the benefit, then proceed to pay full price.

Patience. Imagine flying with an impatient pilot who ignores instructions from the control tower to circle in a holding pattern until further notice. If she yields to the mounting frustration caused by delays and decides to descend towards her destination and force her way onto the runway… the pending carnage would be catastrophic.

We all want green lights, but the Great Traffic Controller also uses stop signs to save us and others around us—that is, if we patiently pay attention. Who knows if you're next, but you'll never know if you act out of turn. Patiently queuing up in a holding pattern guarantees your arrival. Losing your patience simple leads to losing out, period.

Submission and co-mission. A surgeon's expert ability cannot be utilized until the patient yields to the anesthesia to go under the influence. In the same way, going under can refer to submitting control to the Father's skilled touch to remove the pains and stains of our past, the pains and stains that harm us and hold us back.

Submission means vulnerably going under, accepting the mission, and allowing God to step inside our private lives to massage away our mistakes and heartaches. Submission means carrying the mission forward.

But God has gone above and beyond submission; He has called us to co-mission. Increasing the flow of His favor in our lives requires us to reframe what it means to be commissioned by God; instead of laboring on our own, we are joined with Christ to lift the load together. Submission leads to co-mission with your co-carrier, effectively making your yoke easier and the burden lighter.

Daily discipline. Most accomplishments aren't derived from a single stroke of genius. Rather, they come through daily disciplined decisions. The compounding effect of incremental gains leads to the accumulation of huge returns over time.

Albert Einstein referred to the power of compound interest as the eighth wonder of the world, but what would it happen if we actively applied this principle to our time and effort as well? The sum of our existence is the compounded result of our daily decision-making, which either propels us towards our purpose or pushes us further away. The benefits of remaining obedient towards our destiny in the long-term adds up. How long must we remain obedient? That's up to you. Your daily decisions will dictate how much you believe in the gift of purpose God has given you.

Shifting our mindset to embrace difficult situations could be the difference between suffering through or grinding through your circumstance. But understanding who is taking you through your day two will make all the difference. If we view suffering as a punishment for poor decisions, we might be missing the point and negating the grace of the cross. Grinding through means acknowledging our shortcomings and sin by embracing His grace so we can still rise and lay our hands on the prize set before us. Just like a celebrated vintage, we are refined through the grind of our progress, allowing the full body of our taste to develop in flavor and favor.

God is revealing the refined wine being fermented through your day two. Your flavor is compounding in value through the hidden moments of your life so that when God does pour you out, the world will taste and see that the Lord is good.

In between Good Friday and Easter Sunday, Jesus stepped into His future and recalibrated the potency of His name. He confirmed what God had already decided, to usher in a brighter future for our sin-sick natures. He ravaged the enemy, establishing His authority over life and death.

With the keys to open and close doors firmly in His hands, we can now operate in the places and spaces He has called us into. He was perfectly aware that He would be coming out again, but He knew there would be no day three resurrection without the day two grind. He knew there would be no throne room without the tomb!

CHAPTER FIVE

Life Is Like a Fast Food Combo

Where there are no oxen, the manger is empty, but from the strength of an ox come abundant harvests.

(Proverbs 14:4, NIV)

Like **many families** growing up in my generation, fast food was a staple of the weekly menu. You could say that the Colonel, Wendy, and Ronald with the big red shoes were all close family friends! A cheeseburger kids meal was always my go-to. I was never big on fries, but I had no choice but to eat them; we were taught to never leave food on our plate. Not until I'd eaten *all* my food was I allowed to have the best part of every combo: the surprise gift/toy that came inside! The fries were the price to pay, but they were always worth the reward.

With my daughters, I still enjoy frequenting drive-thrus, and to this day I still order the same kids meal although I adult it by adding lettuce and tomatoes to my burger. I exchange the soda for water, but I am yet to develop an appreciation for fries. These days you have options, so I always ask them to hold the fries and swap it out for apple slices. But inevitably they still drop fries in the bag too!

On one particular lunch trip through the drive-thru, my oldest daughter sensed a measure of annoyance percolating in me as I once again found fries in my bag. She forever shaped my outlook by saying, "Dad, that's just how combos are built."

In that moment, the seeds for this chapter were sown. Life is not like a box of chocolate; life is like a combo… whether you want them or not, you are getting fries with that. What's the price you have to pay to get the reward inside?

Jesus doesn't mince words. In John 16:33, He states that in this world we will have trouble but to gird up our focus and tenacity and take heart. We can overcome the trouble that is bundled into this life as we pattern the process of progress to overcome the wild ride.

In Jesus, there is no ignorance of the realities we face. In fact, the objective of John 16:33 is to challenge us to reframe our struggles or opposition as opportunities to level the playing field with the right response and perspective. Jesus was levelling out the highs and lows of life when He said in Matthew 5:45 that the sun rises for both the evil and the good and that it pours rain on everyone regardless of how righteous we believe we are. Irrespective of socioeconomic, cultural, geographic exposure, or our collective experiences, we have all been granted the same resource of time and access to God. How we nurture and utilize these gifts determines the depths of faith, joy, and fulfillment we experience.

Whether in work settings, athletics, or leisure activities, we will hear people shout "I was born for this!" when they operate in the sweet spot of their purpose. But before we declare what we were born *for*, we should consider what we were born *with*. Evaluating what you were born *with* acts like a heat-seeking missile that will find its mark to land on what you were born *for*.

Many people struggle with their specific purpose, so instead let's take a few moments to focus on the common gifts all of humanity has received. Consider this: if God gives us a hill and says there is gold in it but doesn't tell us where it is in the hill, is it still enough that He gave us the hill?

How we work the hill is entirely up to us. It plays a greater role in our eternal outcomes than the size of the hill. And how we use the gift of the hill is key to glorifying God. If we pound that rock daily, will we not eventually secure the gold? Being aware of what God has placed in our lives is important to help us activate the universal gifts God has given us.

These gifts represent golden opportunities to uncover and recover what is ours. Swing your axe to chip away the unnecessary to reveal the necessary. Pound the rock with these universally granted gifts.

The grace of the cross. The inherent grace in every sunrise is a built-in reset button to take another swing of our axe to progress in our purpose. Even when we mess up, the grace of the cross allows us to get over it and get on with it.

The cross acknowledges the days when we don't swing, and the cross acknowledges when we swing at the wrong targets. The cross acknowledges the times when we swing with half-hearted effort so we can simply check the box and say we tried.

And then grace provides another sunrise.

The beauty of the cross is that there's no loss! God even redeems the messes we create and His spilled blood redeems, recalculates, and recalibrates our course to point us back on track. But are you actively applying the grace of the cross to your messes and successes? It's in your combo; pull it out.

The ticking of the tock. We often hear people complain about inequities, but we all have access to the same nonrenewable resource of time. We're all afforded the same twenty-four hours per day. This is the greatest equalizer for all mankind.

What time do you wake up? What time do you sleep? Do you *have* time or do you *make* time? Most of us aren't as busy as we make it out to be. If we made the attempt, we could carve out at least five hours a week. That's almost eleven full days per year, or six and a half full workweeks.

If you could carve out five hours a week, the possibilities would be endless. So it's not about having the time; it's about making the time. Time is an inevitable part of life's combo. Put it to use.

The needs/opportunities around us. How fortunate are you that you can be a conduit through which the Father's Kingdom is established? How blessed are you to see the you-shaped requirement of your family, friends, or co-workers? What a privilege it is that your office, church, and community can all benefit from you!

There's no shortage of opportunity if we can just look past the end of our noses and stop navel-gazing at all the problems that plague us. Yes, we are all broken people. So what do we do? How else will you have a story to tell in eternity when you're standing around Peter, Elijah, and Ruth? You'll never know what's on the other side of your obedience until you step out.

That's the opportunity—to discover the value you can represent to others, to be a shelter in the rain and shade on a scorching hot day. Opportunities are in your combo, so be the relief others need in a hurting and broken world.

Free will. To do or not to do is a choice. Everything exceptional we develop in this life took time and a concerted effort to construct. Let's say you do free up those five hours per week, or 260 hours per year. What you do with it would be entirely up to you.

The greatness of any accomplishment is found in the sum of the daily decisions we make in the direction of our destinies. If you choose to use that time towards other endeavors, that's fine. But then don't waste time hoping for something you had the opportunity to progress in but didn't choose to pursue. To gain ultimate fulfillment, it will cost you something. Choose wisely.

⸻ ❧ ⸻

What were you born with and what came in your combo? We're selling ourselves short if we only embrace the good but not the bad and the ugly. God uses all these things to beautify our lives.

Jesus said that on this side of eternity we will have trouble, turmoil, and turbulence… so what are we going to do about it? Paul had a thorn in his side. Joseph and David had haters for brothers. Ruth was left taking care of a widow with no income or clear path to a bright future.

Like these giants, it may not be our fault that we feel blocked. But it remains our responsibility to overcome the turmoil.

We cannot eliminate the pain, but we can ensure that it doesn't stain the other gifts we regularly receive from the Father. And despite the unwanted fries in our lives, it's

> The hill-sized potential of our God-given DNA is packed with golden opportunities. How we diligently mine those opportunities is up to us.

our responsibility to exercise our free will to embrace His grace and chase down opportunities to serve the needs all around us. The hill-sized potential of our God-given DNA is packed with golden opportunities. How we diligently mine those opportunities is up to us. That will determine the depths of destiny we experience. Take a swing and chip away at the hill, because only you can develop you.

Both James and 1 Peter begin in similar fashion, amplifying the same principle—not to despise difficulty and diverse situations. Difficulty is fairly linear in its definition, referring to trials and hardship, but the definition of the word *diverse*, or *various*, is captivating. This concept literally represents the full spectrum of what we face, including the reality that we can face simultaneous trials.

The point is that God is aware of the realities we go through. There is nothing new under the sun, nothing He hasn't dealt with before. We must prepare for predictable problems, true, but we must also prepare for unexpected ones. What about the sudden car accident, getting laid off from your job without notice, or your in-laws dropping by uninvited? Is God's desire for us to respond to these scenarios with a measure of joy as well?

The answer is yes. Even when life blindsides us with financial, physical, or emotional trauma, God is letting us know that we will obtain the strength we need to get through by responding to Him with hope.

Counting it all joy allows us to reframe even the most undesirable parts of our combos. Counting it all joy makes our batteries last longer even when there's no end in sight. Counting it all joy is like medicine for our souls (Proverbs 17:22) when we feel dry and in need of hydration. Counting it all joy provides the strength we need when we're in the thick of our battles (Nehemiah 8:10). It leverages hardship to toughen our resolve and focus on the finish line. It is the assurance and security that this too shall pass as we grow in confidence that God will do what He has said He will do.

Joy is not the opposite of sadness. True joy is a daily choice we make despite the diverse trials we find ourselves in. The perplexing nature of embracing joy in the midst of pain is a strong witness for others. It causes them to question why you have the strength they wish they could have.

The same intense heat that purifies gold in the refiner's fire causes the impurities in our lives to boil to the surface, so we can recognize and address them. Impurities can simply cause us to settle for less than God has for us, allowing destructive habits to persist or character faults to sabotage our progress. The biases, barriers, and blockages that have clogged our drains will keep all the refuse in our systems.

That's why God turns up the heat—so we'll know the truth about the hidden things in our lives. Perspiring in the heat is better than expiring before our due date arrives.

How long will we allow negative behaviors to persist? It's up to us. Or we can allow His perfecting heat to purge us of the issues that plague us and pull us back. So don't pray away the very thing God is using to refine the gold within you. Pray that your patience will outlast the pain so that it can perform its perfecting work.

There are three graduating modes to reframing our trials as we progress through the process of embracing joy in every circumstance.

1. **Survival mode.** The journey begins with knowing that God won't give us more than we can handle (1 Corinthians 10:13). We may feel that if we can white-knuckle

it and just hold on a little longer, God will get us to the other side.

Survival mode is a step up from not believing at all. At the very least, it keeps our hope hydrated until the trial is over.

2. **Tolerance mode.** As we accept that in this world we will have trouble (John 16:33), we find ourselves grinning and bearing it, putting up with life's challenges and hoping that our circumstances will change. We will repeat phrases about God's will, but the real challenge is that we don't know His good and perfect will for our lives. So we accept whatever comes our way as good soldiers, taking orders.

   Tolerance mode is better than survival mode, but there is another gear God is calling us into, where His plans are revealed to us as we embrace the highs and lows.

3. **Ownership mode.** We arrive at this phase when we no longer need to reframe turbulent times because we know that every circumstance and scenario serves the purposes God has placed within us. Taking ownership is about moving forward and rising to the grind regardless of what we face in our daily race. We actively seek out sources of inspiration and search for solutions to keep moving forward.

In ownership mode, we no longer need to explain why tough times visit us. We are full of gratitude for every part of the combo that particular day offers up. We treat every day for what it is—a gift from God to continue to establish His purpose through our lives and for the Kingdom.

Counting it all joy has nothing to do with good or bad days. It's about embracing the good, the bad, and the ugly. It means fully acknowledging that we live in a broken world and then actively seeking out the beauty and opportunity in every trial we face.

A foundational principle of the Christian Business Harvest Network (CBHN), an organization I've been fortunate to help establish to aid people in stepping into their calling via their careers, states that there will always be a byproduct of productivity. Simply drive to work and measure the emissions you create.[10]

We experience this principle about twenty thousand times a day. When we inhale deeply, our bodies will benefit from the incoming oxygen. But after we breathe in the oxygen, we breathe out carbon dioxide, a toxic element if it remains in us.

> Where there are no oxen, the manger is clean, but much revenue [because of good crops] comes by the strength of the ox.
>
> (Proverbs 14:4)

The strength of an ox can plow up dry ground like a hot knife through butter. But when you have to clean out its bullpen, and are subjected to the smell of its byproduct, you will have to remember the gain of its hard work.

---

[10] Yes, I'm fully aware of the existence of electric vehicles, but are you aware of the environmental impact of creating just one of those rechargeable batteries?

After preparing the best meal ever for a friend, someone has to clean the dishes—not to mention the stove. Go ahead and experience the best workout ever, but don't be in a rush to meet up with friends after; you may want to shower first!

The gain of progress is always sweeter as we embrace the pain of the process. We want the gain from the power of an ox but perhaps not the pain of cleaning up the mess it leaves behind in its bullpen.

A quirky way of reframing the byproduct of productivity is considering the idea of manure, which is one of the best fertilizers a field can receive. The next time someone attempts to dump their refuse on your field, respond cheerfully: "Thank you for fertilizing my field!" Remember, even byproducts can bless us when we embrace the right perspective.

> A young woman recently married the love of her life, a farmer who had been working the land from a young age. They were wrapped up in their love and ready to take on the world, no matter where their path led. Life soon brought them back to his roots and the couple moved to the farm where he had spent the majority of his youth. She thought she was in for the beautiful sights of never-ending plains, fresh air, and the freedom that would come from setting her own schedule. As they arrived, the first wave to hit her senses was not an overwhelming sense of love; it was the putrid odor of sweaty farm animals. The smell literally caused her to convulse in dry heaves. And the bugs… oh the bugs! She had signed up for a life with her husband, but not the manure that came with the package. Although she

had signed up for the honeymoon, and the romantic views of a thousand stars at night, something had to break—and she began questioning her decision. But she loved her young husband, and this is what they had agreed to do: build their lives together no matter where life would take them. A short time later, her parents visited. Sure enough, they too were hit by the strong smell of animals! To their horror, they found their daughter cleaning the pig's pen and asked her how she could stand the smell.

"What smell?" she asked in response.

Human nature allows us to adapt to and survive difficult times. But God is calling us to take ownership of our lives so we can experience the fullness of what life has to offer. We can either put up with the situations we find ourselves in or make the most of them. It's a subtle difference, but what side of that coin does your lens see more often? At the very least, adapting to a difficult situation is more palatable than complaining and blaming others.

But there remains another level we can grow into, one that ushers in the opportunity for us to see how to make the most of it. The young woman in this story was able to step into her future as she actively embraced the present moment. Then God provided the grace to allow what had once seemed putrid to become palatable. She embraced her fries and was able to rise above the noise, distractions, and even the smell to focus on what mattered most.

Yes, all things work together (Romans 8:28)—the good, the bad, and the smelly—when we have the right perspective, joyfully reframing the negatives in order to serve a positive outcome in our lives. Life is not like a box full of surprise chocolates waiting for us to sink our teeth into them. Most times the predictability of pain, not the potential of surprise, holds us back. It's easy to blame the unknown and sometimes harder to embrace the known in life's combo.

> Success in most things comes not from some gigantic stroke of fate. But from simple, incremental progress.
>
> —John Maxwell

A fabled World War II story finds Winston Churchill strategizing with his fellow Allied leaders about how to turn the tide in their favor. One of the leaders spotted a fish that had somehow found its way into a pool close to where they were enjoying lunch. They agreed that whoever caught the fish without a net would be determined to be the most brilliant strategist among them.

The first leader decided that massive force was required, so he drew his pistol and unloaded round after round into the water. His lack of success stirred the next leader to jump into the pool and try to catch the fish with his bare hands; he only succeeded in exhausting himself.

Churchill then emptied his coffee mug, rolled up the legs of his trousers, and proceeded to sit beside the pool. He began to scoop water out of the pool with the mug, slowly draining it.

"It may take me all day," he said. "But rest assured, gentlemen, I will catch this fish."

Churchill understood the compounding power of daily actions and knew that his perseverance would end up winning the day.

The process of progress includes your daily grind, where no one sees or seems to care. If something is worth doing, then why the hurry? Like any masterpiece, quality takes time.

Take another look at your combo. Have you found His approval and acceptance yet? It's in there. Do you see the vision and provision for your purpose? And have you embraced the grace for your race? It's all in there.

Countless people are waiting on the other side of your obedience to follow through on providing a solution for a need you were born to meet. Undoubtedly, there will be pain in the process and disappointment on your path. But be encouraged, because your daily grind is pulling the summit closer and closer! This is the gift of life's combo—the joy and the pain, the sunshine and the rain. Embrace it all.

CHAPTER SIX

Cut It Out!

She said, "The Philistines are upon you, Samson!" And he awoke from his sleep and said, "I will go out as I have time after time and shake myself free." For Samson did not know that the Lord had departed from him. Then the Philistines seized him and gouged out his eyes; and they brought him down to Gaza and bound him with [two] bronze chains; and he was forced to be a grinder [of grain into flour at the mill] in the prison. But the hair of his head began to grow again after it had been shaved off.

(Judges 16:20–22)

I'm a fan of basketball on all levels, and throughout my school years the anthem for every player of my generation was "I wanna be like Mike!"[11] So naturally, the ultimate goal for every player was to dunk a basketball. Kids no taller than 5'9" would tirelessly work on their calf and core muscles to increase their vertical

---

[11] "Mike" being Michael Jordan, of course, the second best player to ever grace the court. DM me if you want to have the LeBron argument!

jump in the hopes of reaching that crowning achievement—to dunk like Mike!

In my grade, the first couple of guys to dunk were immediately elevated to rockstar status! The effort paid off for some, but for most… let's just say that gravity has a special way of keeping us earthbound.

It was a dream of mine to dunk a basketball, but my DNA wasn't built that way. Considering my build and athletic ability, it just wasn't going to happen. I didn't give up exactly, but I did positively redirect my energies towards what I could do—and then I did that well. I had to get to the point of cutting off unfruitful pursuits to align my focus with what I was capable of.

That isn't a lack of faith. However, in a Christian culture where we tend to abuse the phrase "I can do all things," we need to ensure that we don't overinflate hope where it doesn't belong. Powerful personalities will tell you to stand in front of the mirror every morning and tell yourself, "I can do it!" Okay. But what if you legitimately will never be able to deliver on that positive affirmation?

My dad was not a negative person, but he frequently let me know that I talk too much. That was true. He would say I told too many stories. Also true. But then he'd add that I needed to learn how to be quiet. Not so true.

Unintentionally, he was cutting me off from the very purpose I was put on the planet to fulfill. I was born to connect with people and in turn connect them to their callings. When I realized my purpose and began embracing it, that was my slam dunk! I became attracted to actualizing my proverbial slam dunk everywhere I went.

What a rush it is when you feel fully activated and alive, passionately pursuing your purpose!

But then, as it is with all of us, I began to listen to distracting voices leading the choices that pulled me away from my core deliverables. My decisions slowly but surely led me further away from the sweet spot God had lovingly created for me.

Has this happened to you? Maybe your own pride polluted the purity of your purpose. Maybe pleasing others pulled you away, because you wanted to remain relevant and feel wanted – or even needed by others. Maybe for you that voice was someone who carried influence in your life, like a teacher, pastor, or family member. Someone else might have guided you the wrong way, but it's your responsibility to course-correct and get back on track.

The entrepreneurial life, for example, is not for everyone—and yet people who demonstrate a strong drive are encouraged to start businesses. Why do more than ninety five percent of small businesses fail every year? Why do more than ninety-nine percent of student athletes not make it to the pros?

> if you succeed at the wrong things, you're failing already.

Motivational speakers will inspire you and say that failure is not an option, but I want to reinforce something: if you succeed at the wrong things, you're failing already.

⸻ ❖ ⸻

Samson woke up and got out of bed like every other day of his life, but his life was about to change. As a child, he had been anointed to judge and lead Israel. Bound by a Nazarite vow, there were certain pleasures he could not partake in. The mark of his anointing activated his DNA, and as he grew his supernatural strength became more evident. Samson was born for a purpose!

But the propensities of his unchecked sin nature consistently pulled him away from that purpose. Imagine being the strongest teenager in your entire high school, with a chiseled physique. Imagine getting all that attention, welcomed or not, from everyone. Perhaps the boys wanted to be like him, and the girls wanted to be around him. That type of attention can be hard for anyone to resist.

Before we judge too harshly, ask yourself a question: have you ever fallen to lesser entrapments than Samson? That isn't an excuse for his decisions, but rather an acknowledgement that our daily decisions pave the way towards either our achievement or destruction. Samson's inconsistencies, fueled by misguided pleasures, ultimately pulled him from his purpose. He went from being the chosen one with long, flowing locks to being the chained one, forced to grind wheat all day.

We learn in Judges 16:20 that Samson got up one day, like any other day, but the glory of the Lord had departed from him. His people had written him off, leaving him in the hands of his enemies to suffer for his sins.

But God's mercy never departs. He chased Samson down and built him back up. God's mercies are new every morning, and everyday Samson's God-given DNA vibrated to find a way to renew and reconnect with his purpose. In the end, Samson delivered on his greatness because his DNA would not fail him.

How do you wake up? According to author and researcher Dr. Caroline Leaf, every morning we wake up with new baby nerves that developed while we slept. If these new nerves are engaged immediately, they have the opportunity and ability to take root and join the collective working class of

> The value of anything is in how it is activated, applied, and appreciated.

our brain cells, effectively adding to our capacity. On the other hand, if they're not utilized, they die off and do so quickly.

Lamentations 3:22–23 tells us that His steadfast faithfulness affords new mercies every morning. Yet we are subject to the old adage that says "Use it or lose it."

The value of anything is in how it is activated, applied, and appreciated. How we apply God's mercies separates us from our past and paves the way for a productive day, which compounds into a brighter future. Activating His mercy causes us to sidestep unhealthy patterns of victimizing ourselves for our sin and failure, leading us to develop a greater appreciation for the work of the cross.

How do you wake up and apply His mercy? For all the drama Samson created, God's mercy never failed him. But because Samson got away with it once, twice, and then over and over as he continued in his sinful pattern, he ultimately began to disrespect the anointing on his life. Simply put, the opposite of use is abuse. If we neglect to apply and appreciate God's mercy to refresh and renew our minds, we are abusing and taking it for granted.

Newer vehicles these days come with a feature called lane departure assistance, which alerts you if the car senses you drifting dangerously close to another vehicle. The requirements of Samson's Nazarite vow were supposed to have served the same purpose for him. But like any sensor, you can turn it off or tune it out. His propensity to continually step out of his lane inevitably caught up to him. Repeatedly getting away with something creates a false sense of empowerment; eventually you'll get caught.

If we fail to appreciate God's mercy, we're left to drift slowly from the center of righteousness by which we are called to abide. And because we get away with our sin a few times, we move from the occasional dismissal of the Holy Spirit's nudging to drowning out God's still small voice on a regular basis. Because we get away with it, we may put in the minimum amount of effort and hope for the maximum payoff.

Like Samson, the handcuffs of continued compromise will arrest you. He benefited from the physical strength he had been provided through his anointing and also reveled in a lifestyle that went counter to the vow he was supposed to honor.

We can easily fall into the same trap that Samson did, thinking we can just get up and handle our business like we always have. But if we continually park God outside, the power inside will evaporate as well. A broken power source cannot be recharged by working harder or throwing money at it. That doesn't address the real mess. We have to take the time to really ask, "How did I get back in this negative cycle?"

> You were running [the race] well; who has interfered and prevented you from obeying the truth? This [deceptive] persuasion is not from Him who called you [to freedom in Christ].
>
> (Galatians 5:7–8)

These verses are not a statement. They ask a question that requires an answer with our heads up and eyes wide open. Other people will always influence your choices, creating detours that leave you wandering off-course. Whatever is cutting in on you will create unnecessary entanglements that eventually choke you off from the oxygen you require to finish your race.

Nehemiah is the central figure in the book of Nehemiah. He felt an overwhelming burden to rebuild the broken-down walls that surrounded Jerusalem. Years of neglect and destruction had befallen the city under the occupation of the Persian Empire. Nehemiah knew he would be met with opposition, but he followed through on his internal nudge.

As he rallied the people to finish the work, he gave his workers clear instructions to both rebuild the walls and be on the lookout at the same time. So they built the wall with a shovel in one hand and a sword in the other. They weren't going to be caught off-guard. The opposition you come up against might not be as obvious as a punch in the mouth. It's the small indiscretions, delays, and concessions we make that add up to huge problems over time. Like Nehemiah, staying vigilant about opposition will keep us moving in the direction of our destiny.

And like Samson, if we feel like we can get away with something, it becomes easier to stray than to obey the directives we know have been laid out for us. Delilah cut in on Samson and ultimately cut him off from his anointing, lulling him into a false sense of invincibility. The reality is, whoever resolves to last longer usually wins, and when Samson surrendered to Delilah's persistent badgering, he simultaneously surrendered the covering of his vow.

What is your Delilah? What's constantly cutting in and seeking to cut you off from the source of your power? It could be food, sexual impurity, or laziness. Or maybe it's pride, or perhaps the pain of your past. These things can choke out your potential and prevent you from bearing fruit and experiencing freedom.

Mercy is a beautiful and mysterious thing, righting wrongs and keeping us from the consequences we truly deserve. Mercy course-corrects when our lives get off-track.

Delilah cut off Samson's hair, true, but there's a secret you need to be aware of: your hair is growing back! Even if you fail and fall short, no one can cut you off from the regenerative and restorative power that's stored in your DNA. Samson's superpower was never in his hair but in the God-given DNA that generated his hair!

The Philistines reveled in mocking Samson, but God's timing was about to bring forth Samson's greatest victory. God was building up his strength once again, because His gifts are irrevocable (Romans 11:29). Every morning, God's mercy was restoring and regenerating Samson's strength. With every passing day, Samson's hair grew longer and longer. He could feel the strength return to him, but this time he submitted under God's mighty hand.

God says that He will never reject a broken and contrite heart (Psalm 51:17), so Samson's hair grew back—and so will yours! If the pain of your own poor decisions has destroyed your confidence, your hair is growing back. If words have beaten up your self-esteem, God can redeem your passions and purposes; your hair is growing back! If your mistakes have taken relationships away from you, know that your hair is growing back. You may have let yourself down, but be assured that the DNA God deposited within you will never shrink to the level of your failure; it will always call you higher to the amazing purposes God created you for. Your hair is growing back!

The Gospels mentions four women who didn't settle for the status quo that boxes people in based on age, gender, and ethnicity. They weren't going to be told or pressured to stay in their lanes. These four women experienced the love of God, who mercifully cut off the yokes shackling them to shame. Jesus ushered all four of them into the freedom and liberty we all have access to through Christ. But they had to take action to activate and apply this mercy in their lives.

In **John 8**, an adulterous woman was caught and brought to Jesus to see what He would do. The religious leaders of the day dragged this defenseless woman through the streets for all to see, reinforcing her shame. As judgment was about to fall on her, Jesus cut in on her accusers. He raised a protective standard around her and declared that just because she'd gotten caught didn't mean she would be cut off. The woman's accusers dropped their stones as the flawed nature of their system was exposed, a system in which women receive punishment for a type of crime for which men walk away scot-free. Christ's forgiveness cut off this woman's punishment as she was set free to move forward and sin no more.

Activate and apply forgiveness in your life. All it takes is a simple confession to the Father that we are sinners who accept and acknowledge His mercy.

In **John 4**, a Samaritan woman with a loose lifestyle was drawing water from the same well she had gone to her entire life. Then a Jewish man, Jesus, approached and asked for water. She struggled with the generational hate and disdain her people had received from the Jews. How did this man have the audacity to ask for water?As His words of life quenched her soul, He began to cut her off from her past, offering her a path of reconciliation.

Forgiveness cut her off from her past and set her free to move forward.

If you don't feel free, all it takes is acknowledging that you are already loved and chosen. That's up to you.

In **Luke 8**, a woman with a longstanding and debilitating blood issue was supposed to stay in her proverbial lane, but instead she began to hastily push people aside to cut through the noisy crowd to get to Jesus. She wasn't going to wait for an invitation for her physical liberation that had plagued her for more than a decade.

Her faith to reach out to Jesus ushered in a new era of wholeness and peace. She was set free to move forward. Are you ready to push beyond your past?

In **Luke 7**, a woman with an alabaster jar full of the very perfume she had used to lure men decided to smash the proceeds of her past at the feet of Jesus. The establishment wondered, *"Does Jesus know who's touching Him? If so, He should know this isn't acceptable according to our cultural and societal norms."* She kept her head down to avoid making eye contact with the judgmental eyes staring at her, but Jesus was about to elevate her to heights of historical importance.

She could not and would not wait for a more convenient or appropriate time. Her all-in action in the present cut her off from her past and forever rewrote her future. She had no guarantee how it would turn out, but she knew that she had to pour out! Are you ready?

Homeostasis is a vital and necessary thermostat in our brains that regulates our steady state, such as body temperature. If it's too cold, we shiver, creating kinetic energy to warm us back up. If it's too warm, our sweat glands open up to keep us from overheating. An unfortunate outworking of homeostasis is complacency, as we tend to prefer life to go on without change. If unchecked, this will keep us just the way we are. We get comfortable with being comfortable and make the most of what we already know. Homeostasis can override the promptings and desires in us that says, "There must be more to this." It's the epitome of inertia, which suggests that a body at rest tends to stay at rest. But God is constantly placing pebbles in our shoes. Discomfort isn't necessarily from the enemy; it can be God's way of getting us moving!

We need to get comfortable with being uncomfortable. This is a necessary progression in our pursuit of purpose as we allow God's Word to rewire our thermostats to warm us up to His ever-increasing glory. Get more comfortable being favored over others! At the same time, Get more comfortable with the work it takes to move uphill so you can experience more mountaintop vistas!

What is your immediate next step? What's creating hesitation? What obstacles are in your way? What could be misguiding and misdirecting you? The answers to these questions might be uncomfortable, but that discovery can finally remove the weeds that choke out the seeds that haven't produced fruit in the past.

There will never be a perfect time, perfect price, or perfect place to cut off whatever is cutting you out. And you'll never have perfect agreement from others. It might be uncomfortable and inconvenient, and it may cost you time, your standing at work or with family, and dollars in your bank account. But God is calling you to smash the jars that have held you in shame and break through the barriers that have held you back. He's not going to stop pursuing your wholeness because it's uncomfortable. Cut it out before it cuts you off from moving, from glory to glory.

CHAPTER SEVEN

The Grass Is Greener!

They gave Moses this account: "We went into the land
to which you sent us, and it does flow with milk and
honey! Here is its fruit. But the people who live there
are powerful, and the cities are fortified and very large.
We even saw descendants of Anak there."

(Numbers 13:27–28, NIV)

After finally clearing airport security on a recent international
trip, I found a cozy spot in the boarding lounge with about three
hundred of my "closest friends." As I waited, an announcement
sounded through the overhead speakers: "Attention, passengers:
please ensure your carry-on luggage remains with you and in
sight at all times."

I reached my hand down to ensure that the front zipper of
my carry-on had been closed up after the security inspection.
When they'd asked me whether I'd packed my own bags, I had
answered honestly: "No. My wife did!" I should have known better! That initiated a long and inconvenient search.

But in the end, that search served a greater purpose. I began
to ask—and answer—an important question: "Wait… who *did*
pack my bags?"

Whether by plane, train, or automobile, the opportunity to step outside our regular routines remains a welcome block of time on anyone's calendar. Some enjoy lounging on a beach or by a pool soaking up the sun for hours while others would rather spend their time camping in the backcountry dressed in camouflage with fishing rods in tow.

Neither appeal to my family. Our preference is to set sail on cruise ships and be able to step off the boat in a new port city every day to experience the rich culture and cuisine.

Whatever your form of R&R, the memories we cherish from our time away tends to be selective. Rightly so, we remember the glamorous moments and forget the grinding minutes, or hours, spent during the tiresome process of travel. Our minds extend grace because the destination will be worth it.

Yet we tend to do the opposite in everyday life. Most people focus on the inconvenient parts of their nine-to-five occupations and less on the fulfilling elements of their lives. We measure vacations in moments, but measure work by the minute, hour, and pay period. We hustle for ninety percent of the year to experience a ten percent window to get away from it all. We soon get to the point where we work for forty-eight weeks just to experience four weeks of vacation. This is a problem! We need to flip the script on that math. Life is measured by the moments we create, not by the minutes we consume. A life lived enjoying every day as much as a vacation, is the greener grass worth cultivating. I'm not discounting the concept of downtime, sabbath, or rest. But whether we're on vacation or not, we need to get to a place of making everyday life more fulfilling and memorable. It's about converting our daily minutes into extraordinary moments on par with the joys of going away.

A few years back, we had a neighbor with a corner lot, who diligently watered his grass and manicured the lawn. It stood out so much that the neighborhood pet owners allowed their leashed friends to make it their preferred public washroom! I felt bad for the effort he put into his green grass only to have others dump all over it.

Without trying to incite him, I let him know about what was happening. But he was fully aware of this and was innovatively planning to unleash his inner Thomas Edison. He had rigged his sprinkler system with a remote, allowing him to covertly sit inside his family room with a view of his front lawn.

For the next few weeks, with a smile on his face, his souped-up super-soaker was let loose every time the usual suspects came along. Needless to say, after a few weeks the traffic on his lawn—and the "special packages" being left behind—was cut down significantly.

What do you do when people come by to dump negativity, inferiority, or other unhealthy thoughts on the front lawn of your mind? How long will you let it continue until you do something about it? When will you put up your *No Trespassing* sign?

There are generally four ways we can respond when facing a threat or confrontation: fight, flight, freeze, or fawn.[12] The risk/reward or pain/pleasure scales determine the conviction or intensity with which we step into each of these modes.

---

[12] Mia Belle Frothingham, "Fight, Flight, Freeze, or Fawn: What This Response Means," *Simply Psychology*. October 6, 2021 (https://www.simplypsychology.org/fight-flight-freeze-fawn.html).

For example, if an aggressive dog is moving towards your child, you will spring into action to *fight* back the dog and/or quickly remove your child from danger and take *flight*. The *fawn* and *freeze* responses are both forms of conflict avoidance.

At the onset of conflict, fawners want to please everyone and move quickly to diffuse the situation, but the issue never really gets resolved. It only gets punted further down the road.

In my years of leading sales organizations, the number one challenge my team faced was a customer who delayed or deferred making decisions. This is a freeze response. When we're not willing to make decisions, we freeze up and can't move forward. In the absence of comfort, information, and certainty, many people freeze because their baggage still includes hurt, trauma, and drama. People who are traumatized resist forward motion for fear of having their negative experience repeated. So they seize up, effectively becoming paralyzed while waiting for something or someone else to call the shots.

step forward.

It's up to you to make decisions and take ownership of the health of your grass. You need to decide where your patch of grass is and not be afraid to lay claim to it. Stake your claim and let it be known that dumping on your grass is no longer acceptable.

Is that patch of grass worth the best part of your resources? The decision is yours. If you offend folks with your super-soaker, then offend them, but follow through and let your convictions enforce your eviction notices. Intentionally participate in the process of progress by taking a stand. Fight for your grass. It won't get greener automatically.

⸻ ❈ ⸻

The Lord's Prayer presents a model framework of prayer packed with guidance and goodness. After acknowledging God as our Father, we honor and worship Him as the One who rules from heaven on high. The next line is, *"Your kingdom come, your will be done, on earth as it is in heaven"* (Matthew 6:10, NIV). This suggests a few things. There is a plan, according to His will, that He has laid out—and it includes us as children of our heavenly Father.

In John 15, Jesus says that He shares everything, including His plans for us. Unless we get that into our spirits, we'll accept anything that happens and call it God's will. Unfortunately, many will pray this prayer and never seek out His will for their lives. Absorb the fact that He is more than willing to share His plans with us that He prepared in heaven!

How will we know what patch of grass to water if we aren't asking what to do and where to do it? In the absence of a defined design, our default living blurs out His blueprint. Ans slowly removes his fingerprints from our lives.

As we wander into the desert, losing sight of the long game, our marching song becomes "Que sera sera."; whatever will be, will be. It's easier to assign blame than take responsibility and accountability for our own outcomes. Then we can justify in our own minds why our lands are dry and struggling to produce.

God wants to advance us forward into the promises He has for us. If He didn't, why would He make promises to us? The Lord's Prayer is packed with provision for our journey through life and waters us at every turn. He provides provision for us and then asks us to shed the baggage of the past by forgiving each other and ourselves. This prayer purposely packs our spiritual bags. And because it was intentional, we can call it luggage.

The difference between baggage and luggage, after all, is who packed your bags! Baggage is present when others throw their garbage into our carry-ons, giving us warped and false perspectives. Luggage is present when we pack our bags with intention for the needs we have and the purposes we need to fulfill. Nothing can stop you when your luggage has everything you need in order to pass through a checkpoint, because you took the time to understand what your journey requires.

We convert our baggage into luggage as we set up our own security gates to authorize or deny thoughts the opportunity to take root in our minds, hearts, and spirits. Spending time with God, understanding the truth of who God is and who He created us to be, allows us to separate the baggage from the luggage. Decide if you want greener grass, then unpack your bags and leave the unnecessary behind to make room for the necessary.

The Israelites turned an eleven-day journey into a forty-year adventure, all because they missed their moment. They were headed to greener pastures but taking their scorched earth with them. You can take the boy out of Egypt, but you can't take Egypt out of the boy!

On their way, they were lavished with every material gift possible that their masters had withheld from them. Their bags were fully packed! That was the problem, though: someone else had packed their bags. And so they continued into the Promised Land carrying the baggage of fear and inferiority, continuing on their predisposition toward defeat.

In fairness, we haven't been subject to the torture, travesty, and tragedy they faced. This isn't an opportunity to judge them but to self-reflect. Too many people walk around with baggage other people have packed into their minds, hearts and spirits—including limiting words, traumatic experiences, and self-sabotaging thoughts, to name a few.

Eventually we'll want to venture into greener spaces, but like most growth or advancement, it comes with checkpoints designed to see if we're ready to proceed. If you feel there's a doctor in your DNA, then getting into university and graduating from medical school would naturally be your path. If you want to be a lifeguard at your local pool, you'll enroll in first aid courses and demonstrate your swimming competencies. We must study and demonstrate our competencies to be approved in all areas of life.

A strong desire alone doesn't determine your destination; planning, preparation, and follow-through leads us into the *process of progress.*

Go ahead and put a sixteen-year-old behind the wheel of a race car because they have a strong desire to be a race car driver. What will happen? It doesn't work that way.

You may come to the checkpoint and find that you still believe lies—that your sin is greater than His grace, that you aren't good enough to receive His goodness, or that blessings are only good enough for the bold and beautiful. If so, you might get stuck in line. If the pain of the past still taints your future, then the limiting thoughts you have won't allow you to enter greener pastures.

These checkpoints aren't just hoops to jump through. Rather, they've been set up so that God can give us greater responsibility. By gaining unauthorized entry into places we weren't intended to reach (yet), we can become a threat to ourselves and others. Consider checkpoints to be like reality checks to see what's really in our bags, so that God can fulfill His will and promises in your life and clear you for takeoff. Get ready. There's always another checkpoint around the corner waiting for you to pass through. We can't afford to leave this life to chance or circumstance.

Of the millions of Israelites who set out on that exodus, only two made it to the Promised Land. Only two. I don't believe the rest were all doubters; I believe the majority were easily influenced because they were accustomed to always being told what to do.

Who gets to call the shots and water the gardens of possibilities in your mind? The two who made it all the way, Caleb and Joshua, had a specific ability to bring their own water hose to the party. They had purposely unpacked and left behind the baggage of bondage, leaning into the outlook they had packed in their minds: the potential of possibilities. They embraced the process and saw giants fall limb by limb, one arrow at a time.

In Numbers 13, Moses excitingly selected spies to survey the land God had promised to them. In doing so, we see the planning and preparation that precedes possession. Moses's conviction of God's voice was like history being written in real-time. He knew beyond a shadow of doubt that if God said they would possess the land, it was only a matter of time before they did.

Moses took responsibility to reverse engineer the steps it would take to fulfill his purpose. He was looking for soil, for watering holes and paths to *make* it happen—not to see *if* it could happen.

When the spies returned, their fear, insecurity, and baggage spoke on their behalf. They had been belittled to the size of grasshoppers their whole lives, and that outlook went unchecked as they carried their baggage from Egypt. Their vision was so polluted with inferiority, their fear yelled so loudly in support of their enemies, that they decided the battle was over even before it began. They couldn't reconcile reality and were left wandering and wondering what could have been if only they had believed.

God was inspecting the baggage packed in the hearts and minds of His people then, and He is still examining our beliefs today. Who packed your bags? Be a spy in your own eyes and evaluate what's in your bags. What do you really believe? At the end of our time here on the earth, it will be the systematic thoughts we believe in that either limit or lift us into greener pastures.

Get ready. God is clearing you through the next checkpoint.

Breaking up soil to receive seed requires a stronger force than what we apply in the daily course of life. A certain level of violence is needed to break up the hard ground in our hearts and minds that hardships have caused. This is not gentle Jesus, meek and mild, lying in the manger. This is the side of Christ we see in Revelation 19, where the King of kings comes riding on a white horse with a sword in His hand, eyes like fire with His legs all tatted up. He comes to break the marrow out from bone, to separate truth from lies, light from darkness, and sheep from goats.

We need stronger tools to enforce the eviction notices we've been trying to serve. Ultimately you're responsible for yourself, so assign yourself as the security guard at every checkpoint. If God has given you the authority to trample on snakes and scorpions (Luke 10:19), surely He has also provided the authorization and tools to enforce His will for your life.

Get comfortable with the weapons of your warfare, like prayer. These tools are mighty to pull down every losing thought and make it subject to His will for your life (2 Corinthians 10). When our eyes cannot see the hidden assignments attempting to pass through our gates, trust the silent alarms the Holy Spirit sets off within you. He is the greatest metal detector, X-ray machine, and revealer of truth.

But the simplest of all weapons formed against you is persuading you to water a lawn that doesn't align with your purposes. Certainly, share your resources with others, but not at the expense of losing focus of your own deliverables. It may *feel* right, and it may even have the appearance of godliness, but if the resulting fruit doesn't equal what God is looking for when He passes by your tree, will Judgment Day be in the balance? Weaponize your faith. Weaponize your focus. Redeem the time you are given while you have it.

The grass is greener where you water it. Are the key resources you have in this life flowing to your purposes and watering your grass? Ensure that your time, finances, energy, and relationships all hydrate the dreams God has deposited within you. What tools are at your disposal?

1. **Your Calendar.** As previously discussed, the equation isn't about having time but making time. Just as strong men take the Kingdom of God by force as a treasured prize (Matthew 11:12), our calendars need to be wrestled into submission and populated with growing grass. Everyone makes time for what they value, and your calendar shows what you prioritize.

2. **Your Wallet.** Put your money where your mouth is. Where your treasure is, there will your heart be also (Matthew 6:21). During certain seasons, just bring your five loaves and two fishes. In other seasons, go the extra

mile and lay out a buffet to rival cruise ships! [[Do what you can with what you have while you have it.]] Regardless of the amount, investing in your purposes will always yield the strongest returns in eternity.

3. **Your Effort.** If we simply redirected about five percent of our effort every day towards realizing our purpose, consider what we could accomplish in twenty days! Your effort is solely within your control and should be subject to great evaluation and measurement. Only when we begin to scrutinize it, will we materialize the types of manifestations we feel we are capable of.

4. **Your Relationships.** Our calling calls out for collaboration. Jesus gathered, invested in, and loved on His disciples to ensure that His mission would be established beyond the empty tomb. David had Jonathan to jumpstart his royal ascent, and Joshua had Moses to mentor and model leadership. We all reap what we sow, so if you don't currently have strong guidance in your life, be that mentor to someone else! If you sow into others, God has no choice but to honor that seed and bring the same type of fruit into your life.

The grass is greener where the soil is better. A seed cannot grow itself. It's dependent on pulling nutrients from the soil in which it is planted, a principle that is emphasized in Isaiah 61:11.

During your waking hours, what room in your home do you plant yourself in most? Is it the family room, with remote in hand? Or do you sit at a table, learning new ways to be even better at what you're already better at? At work, who do you gather with most often for lunch, and what is that conversation mostly about?

We control where we park our thoughts and how the soil we reside in will activate the plans within us. There is a correlation between where we park most often and the progress we make in establishing our purpose.

The grass is greener where the atmosphere is better. Atmospheric conditions like rain, pollutants, and sunlight play a role in the health of soil, ultimately impacting the health of a seed. Consider the atmosphere your mind is subject to, and within which your thoughts incubate.

Like fresh rain passing through pollutants in the air to refresh the land, every past experience and media influence acts as a filter through which your thoughts are received. What you allow into your atmosphere becomes your thoughtmosphere—the nourishment of the soil in which our thoughts sit.

We can all go to church on Sunday, but the quality of that experience will be very different based on the atmosphere that nourishes the soil there. What is watering your lawn, and what sun warms up your purpose? What slows you down and freezes you out of your destiny? These questions require an answer, and that answer needs to come from you as the steward of your own existence.

The grass is greener when you use better seed. The best seed is the one that has already been sown! Be selective with the soil and atmosphere, but don't hold back. Better seed is like the widow's last two mites (Luke 21:1–4), [[meaning the seed explodes in value by one's attitude and the heart in which one sows it.]]

Seed becomes better with a willing heart that isn't worried about preservation but rather proliferation, trusting that sowing in obedience to God will always bring about a larger harvest than one's efforts alone could. Better seed is the one that is in your hand right now. It runs the risk of becoming stale and useless if it's not planted. We read in 1 Corinthians 9:6 that an abundant harvest isn't possible when we sow sparingly. Be generous with your seed and watch God multiply it.

The grass is greener when you have a maintenance plan. Within a couple of hours of washing your car, run your hand along the side and you might be surprised that your fingers are already dirty. Our human existence is subject to entropy, and it's a daily responsibility for us to stay sharp. No man knows the time or the hour when Jesus will pass by looking for fruit off their tree (Mark 11), so it's paramount to be prepared in and out of season.

Our daily decisions amount to maintaining our faith and our focus. How we keep our faith strong and our focus sharp will determine how many finish lines we cross.

I pray that it will become your passionate pursuit to develop the grass on your lawn, that it will be you personal pleasure to push past the roaring lion who seeks to steal your purpose, joy, and resolve.

We face real threats, and that's why God graciously sets up security checkpoints to capture every unhealthy thought (2 Corinthians 10:5). These gates are meant to let us in, not to keep us out. They are designed for us to determine how we think and operate, so we can check into the next seasons and stages of our lives.

Going through security with something unauthorized is harmful to you and a threat to others. It's true what we hear at airports: "Attention, passengers: please ensure your carry-on luggage remains with you and in sight at all times." We should be mindful of what goes in and remains in us. It can make the difference between staying grounded and proceeding to the runway, cleared for takeoff.

CHAPTER EIGHT

Embrace the Grace!

Because the Sovereign Lord helps me, I will not be disgraced. Therefore have I set my face like flint, and I know I will not be put to shame.

(Isaiah 50:7, NIV)

Beginning in March 2020, governments spanning the globe struggled to contain the fluid nature of the COVID-19 pandemic. Specifically in Ontario, Canada, smaller retail stores were ordered closed for months on end to stem the burgeoning spread of the disease and minimize contact.

Therein lies the challenge: the government could order a business closed but could not order minds back open when they deemed it was safe to do so. The virus of fear had taken root. They could shut down restaurants, but they could not force confidence back into the hearts of people to go out into public once again. They limited gathering sizes but could not minimize the growing fractures their policies had created in society.

In his book *What's So Amazing About Grace?* author Philip Yancey has this to say:

> A state government can arrest and punish KKK murderers but cannot cure hatred, much less teach them love. It can pass laws making divorce more difficult but cannot force husbands to love their wives and wives to love their husbands. It can give subsidies to the poor but not force the rich to show compassion and justice.[13]

And now society stands more delineated, skeptical, and skewed towards their neighbors than ever before. If we don't agree on policy or politics, can we still be friends? What happened to love thy neighbor, let alone love thy enemy?

Greater isolation has created groups of people labelled *persona non grata*, a military term meaning that a person has been ostracized. It is a person who is unacceptable or unwelcome and therefore rejected by society as a whole. Yancey goes on to say that someone labelled *persona non grata* is literally "a person without grace."

In historical terms, leper colonies created many people who were *persona non grata*. They could no longer receive space or acceptance. In the Indian caste system, groups known as dalits and pariahs are known as untouchables. They experience fierce rejection and isolation— and in some cases, even worse outcomes. When we become selective in the quantity and quality of grace we give, we can to a point where people live in disgrace.

If we don't develop an understanding of grace's close cousin, mercy, we are left with additional blinds spots. The definitions of mercy and grace vary slightly, but significantly. Mercy is not

---

[13] Philip Yancey, *What's So Amazing About Grace?* (Grand Rapids, MI: Zondervan, 1997), 251.

getting what you deserve and grace is getting what you don't deserve. The sweet spot between these two is the cross, where the greatest act of mercy and grace took place. In Christ's crucifixion, we don't deserve the sacrifice of God's only begotten Son, yet by grace Christ was fully given as an atonement for our sins.

Fundamentally, for the work of the cross to be complete, every believer must set aside every hindrance to embracing the gifts of the cross. In Greek, the word for grace is *charis*, which means to "rejoice in what affords you joy. It is gladly receiving unmerited favor and the benefit despite the doubt."[14] Shattered self-esteem, guilt-driven gluttony, and BS (blame and shame) constantly limit our ability to rejoice in receiving the fullness of His goodness.

Perhaps others have treated you like persona non grata, or maybe you've felt like a pariah. Check to see if these limiting perspectives are holding you back from embracing His grace. We don't deserve mercy or grace, yet because we are called to pick up our cross daily (Luke 9:23) we have no choice but to fully embrace the grace afforded by the cross. Are you getting full value out of your decision to follow Jesus? Embrace it. All of it— that which you don't deserve and the mercy that pardons you from what you do deserve.

As parents, my wife and I hope that our daughters will recognize, and eventually appreciate, the intentional guidance, approach, and concessions we offered according to their individual personalities. At times the discrepancy in our parenting has been met with exclamations of "That's not fair!" Our response?

---

[14] "Charis," *Studylight.org*. Date of access: January 16, 2023 (https://www.studylight.org/language-studies/greek-thoughts.html?article=30).

"You're right!". Who told you that life was fair? Who told you that life would come with a great equalizer for all to partake in uniformly? We have all been afforded very different starting points by way of family, freedoms, and finances. The history of the world has shown that we will always have the poor and the rich among us.

Embracing what's in your own wallet demonstrates gratitude for the sacrifices He made on the cross. Gratitude allows us to operate in peace and security regardless of where you find yourself on the economic scale. Thankfulness causes us to focus on what we have versus what we don't have.

I would rather have five loaves and two fishes that God can unlimitedly bless others with versus striving to accumulate storehouses on my own that moths and rust will eat away anyway (Matthew 6:19).

Keep your eyes on your own prize.

Does it bother you that some people can eat a couple of cheeseburgers and immediately go out and play football while others seemingly put on weight by simply looking at a piece of cheesecake? Some have a natural affinity for numbers while others should never delete the calculator app on their phone. Some can create mesmerizing and inspiring artwork while others should stick to, well, stick figures! Does God reserve the right to dispense the gift of grace as He sees fit? As we set our focus on the measure of grace already granted to us, instead of the inequalities we encounter, we are put in a ready position to receive greater favor.

We are not called to ignore injustice. Quite the opposite! The point is that we must not allow imbalances, perceived or otherwise, to get in the way of our mission. Sometimes God's grace is the only thing that can get us past those very challenges. You see, we might be praying for more grease to make the path easier while God wants to pour more grace upon us to make us stronger.

Fundamentally, what makes grace challenging is that it cannot be measured on a scale of justice. The parable about workers in a field in Matthew 20 shatters many of our norms around fairness. Some workers were hired first thing in the morning and agreed to their wages. Another group was hired midday and agreed to be paid what the landowner decided. Then a third group was hired closer to the end of the day. At the end of the workday, all three groups received the same wage!

In his book, Yancey tackles the themes explored in this parable:

> Jesus' story makes no economic sense, and that was his intent. He was giving us a parable about grace, which cannot be calculated like day's wages. Grace is not about finishing last or first; it is not about counting. We receive grace as a gift from God, not as something we toil to earn, a point that Jesus made clearly through the employer's response.[15]

Again, does God reserve the right to dispense the gift of grace as He seems fit? You cannot fully embrace what is yours until you take our eyes off what God gives to others. The deceptive nature of envy is that it will seek to fill the void and erode your ability to embrace your own grace for your own race.

---

[15] Yancey, *What's So Amazing About Grace?* 61.

What is balance and what is justice? That God should sacrifice His only begotten Son? Where is the equality in the torture He endured so you and I could have the crippling weight of sin lifted off us? We can never repay the Trinity in full, so how do we transcend the normal conventions of give and take? Even if we tried, we couldn't make two and two equal four on our own, not if we were weighed on the scales of holiness. According to God's math, however, five loaves plus two fishes does not equal seven. It equals more than five thousand!

With God's grace, what could your two plus two now equal? Grace allows us to flourish even when our thoughts, actions, and output do not equal righteousness.

Judas was the bookkeeper for Jesus's ministry, and he struggled with the scales of give and take within himself. He thought Jesus wasn't allocating the resources properly. You can hear his crooked nature screaming, "That's not fair!" And he was right. He was justified according to his own measurement, but his scale lacked grace. In the end, this cost him more than just a bag of Pharisee silver. A life lived without embracing grace could cost you Eternity.

Considering the cross, I question the concept of fairness and instead appreciate what I do have and seek out greater grace. Thankfully, God loves us based on who He is, not who we are. This world cannot be saved, nor can our lives be reconciled, by balancing the books. Embrace grace.

Most times when I travel, the name of the game is "Hurry Up and Wait!" I wait for my Uber to get to the airport. On the way, I then wonder if I've left anything behind. I rush over to the check-in counter… then wait in line. With boarding pass in hand, I rush over to the security checkpoint to… wait in line (and hopefully not be "randomly" selected this time). I get to the boarding gate and… wait. They announce the flight is boarding and… I wait in line to board. Then there's the waiting for takeoff, waiting to land, waiting to exit the plane, and finally waiting for my luggage! And then, wait… where do I wait for my Uber pickup?

Like most destinations in life, we don't get to choose our cadence or pace—but if we're patient, we will arrive.

Saul faced this challenge. Before going out to war, kings were instructed to wait for the priest to make a sacrifice (1 Samuel 13). Saul's impatience got the best of him and it cost him everything. He decided that he had this in the bag and went ahead to do that which was reserved for the priest. Despite every effort, from that moment on the throne slowly slipped out of his grasp.

Embracing grace includes embracing patience. Rushing our way through life's challenges produces unhealthy perspectives. It creates a dependence on yourself rather a codependence with God.

Impatience generates a negative response when you see someone who started after you, someone who's on a similar journey, get ahead of you. If unchecked, jealousy creeps in when we see someone else appear to walk in the same destiny God has outlined for us.

Imagine the consequences if we, like Saul, got jumpy on a flight and pressured the pilot to immediately land the plane without proper clearance from the air traffic control tower. The carnage could be catastrophic. The pace of our race must be embraced. When we're going too slow, grace can replace the jumpiness we're all prone to feel. When life speeds up to the point that we feel overwhelmed, again grace can pace our response to help us avoid the stresses that may ensue.

Embracing grace means embracing the security and certainty that what God has for you is for you! We don't get to control our ETA, but we do get to control our ability to grow through every moment and infuse joy into our journeys. If you feel like your dreams and desires are delayed, be careful not to sabotage your destiny, because running low on patience generally leads to cashing out way too early.

Embracing grace is demonstrated not in how we act, but more so in how we react when someone abruptly cuts us off in traffic. Or when the person in front of you at the grocery store has already paid but decides to engage the clerk in a conversation about the flowers. Or when you're in a hurry and the driver in front of you fails to understand that there's a minimum speed on the highway![16]

When grace governs our reactions, we keep more of our peace, and we'll pass more tests, allowing us to progress deeper into our purposes.

Growing up I would hear, *If something is worth doing, then it's worth doing well.* I was raised to only celebrate completion and perfection, not progress or small wins. It was all or nothing.

Most of my life, all I had was my five loaves and two fishes. It never seemed like enough, nor did it seem like it could ever *be* enough, to help me reach the heights of my capacities. Other people had goals on their to-do list, but as a young man in my twenties, goals were simply pipedreams that remained on my wish list. So I went about busying myself satisfying other people's needs and

---

[16] Full disclosure: when my wife sees me writing about being patient while driving, the word *hypocrite* might cometo her mind. So please remind her to be gracious towards me. I am work in progress!

experienced only empty satisfaction. Deep down, I knew it was wrong, but now I carried the weight of not letting other people down in the name of Christianity. I knew this type of existence was vacant and void of personal purpose, but at the time it seemed to me that any form of self-worth was better than none at all.

Then it happened. A few years ago, while sitting in the front row of church on a typical Sunday, God asked me to put everything down. My immediate response? *"Get the behind me, Satan!"* But those prompts never went away; they only became stronger and clearer.

At the time, I was a pastor at one of the most prominent churches in arguably all of Canada and God was calling me to put it down. A significant part of my identity was wrapped up in that role. To step away would mean stepping away from everything I had become.

Months later, in the moment when I finally walked into the senior pastor's office to inform her of my decision to step down, grace flooded my soul. I didn't fully understand my next steps, but grace allowed peace to override my need to comprehend what my human existence could never make sense of.

I embraced God's grace that day. God knew I wouldn't understand, but His grace could be found in growing my trust in Him. He was removing the form of godliness I had wrapped myself in by keeping up appearances. I was looking the part and playing the part, but inside I had fallen apart. We can be quick to add a coat of varnish to make us look glossy and brilliant. However, in my case, the outward varnish had actually tarnished the beauty that God needed to bring out of my soul.

From that moment on, grace allowed me to embrace the process of progress. This is critical. I began to be gracious towards myself. I graciously applied patience like a daily ointment. I graciously stopped allowing the act of people-pleasing to drive my decisions, and grace allowed me to stop valuing myself based on the needs I could meet for others. Grace replaced the wiring in my mind that said, "If something is worth doing, then it's worth doing well." My new approach: "If something is worth doing, then it's worth doing poorly until I get better and better."

Understanding how to be gracious towards ourselves helps us understand how to be gracious towards others. Our capacity to love God must be evidenced by our capacity to be gracious towards one another. This life is not about receiving equal gift-ings. It's about what you do with the gifts, talents, and opportuni-ties presented to you.

There is a simple principle: we reap what we sow. How are you demonstrating mercy towards your co-workers and fellow church members? Are you known for being gracious towards family and friends? Intentionally administer grace by design until it becomes second nature. Living ungraciously is venomous and causes you to always look for who's at fault. Human nature avoids humilia-tion and covers up shame, making it easier to blame someone else rather than take responsibility for your own outcomes.

The blood of the lamb can repel shame and disgrace (Isaiah 50:7). And because we reap what we sow, the more gracious we are with others, the more we can expect the grease of God's grace to lubricate the sticky parts of our lives. Expect the grease of His grace to cause your dry bones to rise and dormant dreams to be revitalized.

> Our capacity to love God must be evidenced by our capacity to be gracious towards one another.

Consider who you could and should be more gracious towards, not based on whether they deserve it. No one really does. No one is really worthy. But Jesus even extended grace to the very ones who drove the nails into His hands. Grace allows us to filter through the pain, adversity, and injustice that inevitably visits us all. The scars of trauma can either scandalize or galvanize us. But the grace of God allows for forgiveness, healing, and restoration. The choice to embrace grace is yours.

A young woman was engaged to an honorable man close to her hometown. She had been prepared for this moment for most of her teenage years and felt safe and secure in the strength of his arms. He was an upstanding gentleman and they looked forward to building a life together.

"Pregnant? What do you mean, I'm pregnant?" she cried out to an unknown presence. "How will my fiancé react and how will we handle the shame and disgrace to follow?"

Mary and Joseph had a choice. They could allow the scenario to scandalize them or galvanize their resolve. The scandal in grace is that we don't get what everyone expects we deserve. Grace provided a Joseph for Mary. Grace also provided a whale for Jonah and a ram for Abraham.

Will you allow grace to deliver what you don't deserve? Embrace it. Embrace His mercy and give yourself permission to move forward. God already has. The fullness of your purpose awaits.

A few years back, while at a local hardware store, I picked up some lawn bags to collect the leaves that were beginning to fall from the trees in our yard. I've always been a sucker for a good sale—and there it was: a shiny, sleek, and absolutely savage power drill! Did I need it? Maybe not, but it was on sale. And did I mention it was shiny? Well, a year and half later, it was still in the unopened package where I keep my other seldomly used tools.[17]

You see, when we have a form of godliness, we deny the real power He has called us to operate in (2 Timothy 3:5). Grace is a power tool that firstly requires us to open it up. That's what this chapter is all about. Why settle for a screwdriver when you can upgrade to a power drill? Grace also upgrades hammers into jackhammers and allows your five loaves to feed five thousand. The tools you've used in the past may have served a purpose, but are you ready to step into a new season with more power? Plug into the power source of grace!

I was studying at a local coffee shop one day when a warning popped up on my laptop: "20% battery remaining." I had to move from the comfy cushioned seat to a hard wooden chair adjacent to a cold window in the middle of winter. But that's where the power source was. It didn't matter if I was happy or not. That's where the power socket was.

Being cranky or grumpy isn't a natural disposition. Do you get mad at the drop of a dime or get tense easily? Do people avoid you? If so, then you need to either take a nap, have a snack, or you to need to gas up on grace! Grace is the power to convert your gifts, opportunities, and regular tools into power tools. To reject grace is to deny the power God offers. If we deny grace, we will continue living in a form of godliness. It may be uncomfortable but get plugged in to the power source.

---

[17] Facebook Marketplace is my wife's partner in shrinking my stockpile of unnecessary shiny purchases!

The *charis* of Christ overrides every crisis that shame would try to saddle you with. So rejoice in what affords you joy and gladly receive His unmerited favor. God's grace placed coins in the mouth of a fish (Matthew 17:24–27), massaged away social distancing protocols as Jesus communed with and healed lepers, and allowed Moses to take a peek into the Promised Land.

What gracious purpose has been prepared for you? Since this can be a long journey of becoming what God has intended, be happy at every moment. If you're waiting until you achieve ultimate success, you might only be happy when you're dead! Enjoy the journey. Enjoy the hiccups, the winding path, and everything in between. Enjoy and embrace the benefits of His grace.

CHAPTER NINE

Two-Factor Authentication

Do not conform to the pattern of this world, but be transformed by the renewing of your mind. Then you will be able to test and approve what God's will is—his good, pleasing and perfect will.

(Romans 12:2, NIV)

A **close friend of mine** has been in the mortgage business for the better part of twenty years. He doesn't feel like he's in the finance business, though. He strongly believes that he's in the home ownership dream fulfillment business! His role is to effectively size each client's dream to their true capacity to both afford and enjoy the largest financial decision they'll ever make.

An early step in the process is securing a loan preapproval to help the prospective new homeowner gauge their buying power. With that validation in hand, he sees his client's confidence soar as they search the market for homes, knowing full well what's within their price range. Because they're certain of their preapproval, they approach the buying process with the assurance that they can own their own home. Preapproval has that type of power.

What have you, before the foundations of the earth, been pre-approved to take dominion over and possess?

In Matthew 9, Jesus was navigating a flurry of voices seeming to come at Him all once. First, the leader of a synagogue, an institution that had aligned itself against Jesus, approached Him. This leader's voice was laden with humility. In fact, it was the desperate voice of a father whose daughter had slipped from this side of life. Helpless and confused, the man had turned to the very one whom his fellow religious leaders were trying to condemn!

But, you see, God will not despise a broken and contrite heart. The desperate prayer of this father shifted the whole scene and soon Jesus and His disciples were all on the move to this man's house.

What needs to shift in your life? What intervention do you need that will only be resolved if God steps in?

Later in Matthew 9, Jesus found Himself in the midst of a fluid crowd, moving with everyone to a rather important date with destiny. They were on their way to the house of this religious leader, whose daughter had died.

Along the way, a woman's voice called out: *"If I only touch His outer robe, I will be healed"* (Matthew 9:21). Jesus turned, wanting to know who had the audacity to follow through on their inside voice and reach out to touch Him. Did Jesus ask curiously? Was He upset or did He feel inconvenienced? I believe He excitedly sought out the person who touched Him and was eager to identify the one who pulled virtue from Him.

The disciples were left confused, as though to say, "Come on, Jesus. We're among a throng of people… and You want to know who touched You?"

Yes!

An interesting thought to consider: of all the people who surrounded them, why did these two people—the religious leader and the woman who reached out to touch Him—captivate Jesus? Neither of them had been granted permission but they both sidestepped any sabotaging internal voices that would have cut them off from their pursuit. Their tenacity and audacity got the attention of Jesus. You too can shift your reality by praying with humility. God is faithful to do His part, but are you ready to do yours? What's your next move?

Jesus pressed through the crowd and soon arrived at the religious leader's home. The first thing He addressed was the noise, shutting out all the clamoring negative voices around Him.

There will also be no shortage of unsolicited opinions in our lives, but we need to decide which voice to allow into our deliberations. Some of you have big decisions to make—launching your own business, moving to another company, buying a home, or wondering if he is the one you should marry—and everyone should address the noise before seeking His assurance.

In 1 Kings 19:9, Elijah also found himself in a noisy situation. He was alone, in the cleft of a rock after Queen Jezebel had put out a kill order on his life. Then a huge tornado hit—but Scripture says that God was not in the wind! Most people would have already interpreted this massive show of nature to have been God moving in vengeance—but no, the tornado was not God.

Next, a massive earthquake struck. But Scripture says that God was not in the earthquake either! What type of response are you looking for? How is God supposed to respond?

Finally, a third phenomenon befell Elijah. Fire fell all around him, but he knew better than to get distracted. Instead he waited on God's voice.

Far too often we get riled up by a frenzied crowd, natural signs, or charismatic preachers, but God is not about that. He's looking for people who are reaching out to Him and actively waiting and listening with dependency on His grace.

Too many people find comfort in the crowd because of the safety of a wider path. The majority couldn't be wrong, could they? The minority, however, has the capacity to shut down public opinion. They have the audacity to desperately chase down God, regardless of how they appear in the process. The minority has the tenacity to push past the crowd and the noise.

The voice Jesus is seeking is yours. He responded to the audacious actions of a woman who wanted to be made whole. He rerouted His plans with the tenacious touch of a father's love. Sometimes we feel the need to move mountains, but I assure you that you have something greater—the capacity to move Jesus. More importantly, He is willing.

How desperate are you? Elijah avoided the noisy distractions of literal earthquakes, wind, and fire but trained his ear to listen for God's still small voice. How determined are you to listen for the One voice that really matters? This is critical, because a successful Judgment Day is all about aligning our lives in pursuit of what He pre-approved for us before the foundations of the earth. He responds and allows virtue to flow from Him with a voice of faith, humility, and certainty.

⚬ ⋯⋯⋯⋯⋯ ⋟•⋞ ⋯⋯⋯⋯⋯ ⚬

In 2010, the storied rivalry between the Los Angeles Lakers and Boston Celtics wrote a new chapter as they played for yet another

NBA championship. In the closing moments of the deciding game, the player formally known as Ron Artest shot and made the dagger three-point shot that ultimately led the Lakers to victory, winning the Larry O'Brien trophy.

Reporters asked Artest afterwards how assured he had felt while taking that shot. For context, his teammate Kobe Bryant, the late, great Black Mamba, had been on the court with him. It had taken a lot of nerve to take that shot instead of putting the ball in the hands of the best player on the court.

His reply to those reporters remains legendary. He said that he heard his coach's voice in his mind. Then he heard his psychologist's voice. And finally, his own. All the voices led to a single choice: *Do I shoot the ball?* That shot was arguably the most critical of the 2010 NBA finals and certainly the most important one of his life.

He was a professional basketball player who had probably taken that shot thousands of times. So why had there been any internal deliberation for that split second? Would Kobe Bryant approve? Would his coach approve? Would the fans and TV commentators approve?

Far too often, seeking approval becomes the determining factor for us. But Ron Artest gave himself the green light on the largest stage he would ever play on. He gave himself permission based on his preparation, based on the story he had rehearsed in his head over the years of taking and making a championship-sealing shot. After all the practice he'd put in, taking rep after rep, drill after drill, shot after shot, in that moment he still had to make a choice.

He gave himself permission. Will you?

Do not conform to the pattern of this world, but be transformed by the renewing of your mind. Then you will be able to test and approve what God's will is—his good, pleasing and perfect will.

(Romans 12:2, NIV)

This verse is a critical bit of guidance to trade our trash for truth. We need to constantly renew our default patterns and reset our "stinking thinking." Whether the influences we normalize and absorb as truth are geographical, cultural, or social, we are all subject to modelling the behaviors we have been nurtured by.

The first sentence of this verse is transformative on its own—and it's been popularized for good reason. But let's for a moment focus on the second sentence. Why does God ask us to approve His will?

…Then you will be able to test and approve what God's will is—His good, pleasing and perfect will.

(Romans 12:2b)

Regardless of what translation you prefer, why does God ask *us* to approve of *His* will?

In sport or corporate settings, team-building exercises are essential for players and employees to come together around the organization's guiding philosophies and culture. As team members, we begin to take ownership of the overall strategy. Coaches and leadership teams will refer to this as buy-in. It means we put skin in the game when a loss is no longer acceptable and the only thing that matters is securing the objective.

In Genesis 11, God looked down and saw the people building the tower of Babel. He then declared that nothing would be withheld from them. This conclusion came in response to the individual people moving as one, with one mind and one voice. The unity of many working together for a common cause is like the percussion in an orchestra flowing harmoniously with the strings and wind instruments.

Now picture that same poetry in motion within your own soul as your purpose aligns with your passion. God is telling us right now to approve His good, pleasing, and perfect will. Until you do, you'll be stuck in old patterns of layering good works and effort on top of faulty foundations. You aren't here to simply serve other people's needs and do good deeds; you are here to live on purpose for a mutually approved purpose.

Approving God's will for our lives generates the necessary buy-in. Have you bought in to His plans for your life yet? Have you considered the cost and put your wallet, calendar, and relational equity behind it? Until you do, you'll serve others' needs and avoid living on purpose.

Approval will require taking inventory of the giftings God has given us and how they can be best used to build greater glory. Even on a good day, most people avoid spending time in front of the mirror because they're prone to seeing their own flaws, scars, and deficiencies in their reflection—or at least, their interpretation of their reflection. What you see in the mirror is up to you, but at what point will you renew your view to see the powerful overcomer God sees you as?

Buying in means believing that the beauty in the mirror is more than enough. Until you give yourself the stamp of approval, you won't be able to approve God's plan and buy in to His design.

This isn't about being good enough or qualified. The Bible says that our best works are filthy rags in His sight (Isaiah 64:6).

Approving God's will for our lives is even more beautiful because we recognize that we aren't qualified but still choose to believe we can fulfill the purposes we feel that God has deposited within us, simply because God said so.

Approval begets buy-in and buy-in begets ownership. When you move in ownership of your purpose, it gets you up early and keeps you up late. It eliminates the elements that so easily fracture our focus.

This entire book so far has led to the point where you need to decide whether you will own your purpose and passionately pursue it. When you own a problem, you can own the solution. When you own the responsibility, it creates the necessary accountability for the outcome. And when you own your outcomes, every step you take will lead in the direction of your destiny.

Ownership unlocks and unleashes the conviction in your core that you've been longing for. Ensure that you don't confuse approval with tolerance, acceptance, or simply the absence of opposition; it's easier for the enemy of your soul to tolerate good deeds and let the world accept a lower-case version of you without creating any ripples. If we sit back and nest in a truncated version of ourselves, we have already lost.

The mere fact that you're on the planet suggests that you have already been pre-approved by God. But this life requires two-factor authentication, and the second stamp of approval is yours to give. Being in the crowd, or even the congregation, can at best expose you to Jesus, but He desires that you experience Him. Your purpose is awaiting your stamp of approval. Through the work of the cross, Jesus signed off on our purpose with His blood-soaked thumbprint, restoring our pre-approval to go take dominion over the land. Will you now sign off with your own blood, sweat, and tears?

In Matthew 16, Jesus asks Peter who the people say He is, but then He tightens the scope to make His point: *"Who do you say I am?"* (Matthew 16:15) As Christians, we most likely celebrate the larger picture of Jesus being the King of kings and we honor the work He completed on the cross. But the question is, who is Jesus to you?

With every new sunrise will come opportunities for our faith to shrink back. Humans have collectively experienced erosions in our faith all the way back to the Garden of Eden. A question was posed by the serpent to Eve: *"Did God really say…?"* (Genesis 3:1) Eve was simply relaxing in the garden when this subtle seed of doubt got impregnated in her belief system.

In the court of law, you need not prove that someone is innocent or guilty; the only proof required is to present reasonable doubt of their guilt so that a conviction cannot be made. The serpent is still whispering, "Did God really say you can succeed in that field? Did God really say you will marry the right one? Did God really tell you to get out of that neighborhood? Are you really good enough or worth enough?" The serpent never came at Eve in full force; he just sowed seeds of doubt. She lingered on these lies, like water to the seed, until she questioned everything she had always held as truth.

Eve's gift of free will became a curse to us all, as she didn't handle her liberty well. Could God have stepped in? Of course, but then He would have violated His own principles of relationship—trusting and having faith in one another.

You'll often hear people say, "I'm just following the Lord's calling." If God gave us free will, why would He want us to robotically "just follow"? Our design suggests that we have the opportunity to choose to be involved, which means that we take ownership of our decisions to progress in our purpose. Taking ownership invites us to be co-laborers with Christ.

If we respond robotically, we create for ourselves a ready-made excuse if a less than favorable outcome occurs. But when we actively participate in the process, we're saying, "God, come hell or high water, I am all-in to establish Your Kingdom through the purposes you sent me to the planet to fulfill."

The night Jesus was arrested, He wrestled with the brutality He was about to face on the cross. His directives were clear to Him, but we should be clear that His struggle was not with the devil; His struggle was with Himself… to own what He was about to face and move forward into His purpose.

You are going to face those moments, perhaps a few times in your life. Your desire will be obedience but being ready to co-sign the work you've been assigned is what will make your moments matter. Is your pen ready?

Don't let the names people call you drown out the name God has given you. Where do you look for approval? From parents, a boss, or friends? In most cases, it's not people's opinions that matter but how much you value their opinion.

How high are your own approval ratings in your eyes? According to the Romans 12:2, that matters more. Some people feel written off because of their past decisions, and because of how others have subsequently treated them. If people want to broadcast your past, most times it only speaks to their own insecurities and inability to move forward.

As you identify your identity to be more victor than victim, you will begin to reframe every situation as serving you, not hurting you You'll see yourself as the rich getting richer, diminishing your doubt and making you feel more assured.

But this beautiful exchange will cost you something. Maybe everything you have previously defined necessary. What valuable endeavor has the price tag scared you from pursuing? Dream again and believe again. It's not arrogance to give yourself permission to be as great as possible; it's assurance—blessed assurance that you have been made in the great image of a great God!

Is the drive to become everything God has for you worth it despite trials and tough times? You prove your answer every day by giving yourself permission to move forward even when the conditions aren't ideal, even when voices around you might be saying "You can't! You shouldn't! Who do you think you are?" Are you ready to tell—or rather, show—the world who God says you are?

My prayer is that this book helps you discover, recover, and reinforce your path and purposes set out for you through His will. It's about understanding that challenges aren't meant to *define* us, but rather to *refine* us. It's about looking at your past not as a problem, but a propeller to move forward.

Have you committed murder? Moses did. Have you committed adultery? David did. Have you walked away from Jesus? Peter did. Reframe what you used to be and what you used to do as simply something that built your character and caused you to course-correct. Our past prepares us for our potential. Nor does it diminish the destiny loaded in our DNA. Will you free yourself to blast through the chains and pains of your past to approve His good and perfect will for your life? That active choice is fifty percent of your contribution to the equation.

Free will is the beauty in God's design that completes the two-step authentication of our purpose as we approve His good and perfect will for our lives. What you freely choose to buy into really is up to you. The choice is yours. Your eternity depends on it.

CHAPTER TEN

Faith Is in the Follow-Through

For just as the [human] body without the spirit is dead,
so faith without works [of obedience] is also dead.

(James 2:26)

I may not have been the next legendary basketball coach like Nick Nurse, but I was fortunate to be a part of my daughter's teams as an assistant coach for a few years. She spent hours and hours working on her shot release to develop the muscle memory required to make shooting instinctive. This earned her a reputation as a sharpshooter.

Technically speaking, before a player takes a shot, they're taught to create space to get the shot off. Once you release the ball, you follow through on your shot with your wrist in the same way you would with your golf swing or slapshot in hockey.

Upon release, my daughter could generally sense if the ball was going in. And if it was off, she would immediately follow her shot to try and get the rebound. She learned that even the best shooters miss. But more importantly, even if you miss, perseverance always creates another shot opportunity. Follow your shot.

One of the greatest lessons she in turn taught me was this: *"Your belief is tested before fruit is manifested."* She showed herself and God that her faith had the endurance to last through the tough times that invariably visit us all.

We need to learn how to trust the process. For my daughter, this meant trusting that her work would pay off. She had to trust that God honors and rewards those who diligently pursue what He calls us to do in every season.

Even more importantly, she taught me that the journey of faith is not complete until you possess your promise. When doubt attempts to erode your faith, hold your shot and follow it. The fullness of faith is in the follow through… until you possess your promise.

We can all feel like the two blind men who followed Jesus in Matthew 9:27–29. We stumble around, trying to figure out where to go to school, who to marry, or even what to order off the menu! Answers are comforting, yet if we had all the answers, we wouldn't need faith.

If I'm honest, I have settled for less than the fullness of what faith could deliver more times than I wish to count. Instead, I chose that which was familiar, comfortable, and convenient.

In 2 Corinthians 5:7, we are encouraged to walk by faith and not by sight. In Matthew 9, Jesus asked two blind men, whose entire lives were predicated on faith and not by sight, whether they believed. They literally lived out that scripture everyday of their lives. They had to trust the footing of their next step without seeing it. They had to trust that the food going into their mouths was consumable. They had to trust that no one was taking advantage of them. Their entire world was a function of walking by faith and not by sight.

Yet Jesus still asked them to step into another dimension of faith they had never expressed or experienced.

You most likely believe that, in general, God can make all things possible. But Jesus was asking a different question, and He's still asking it: do you believe God can make your dreams and desires a real possibility for you? A successful Judgment Day means exercising the type of faith that says His promises are for *you*. We need to faithfully live while knowing that the God who made the universe is for us and has our back. The glory of the cross is for everyone, as He had each of us in mind, including all the shame and pain we carry.

Faith is how we show up, even after we miss out or mess up. Trusting the process of our faith journey is not a singular moment in time. It unfolds in stages, moving us from promise to possession. For most, it begins with a word from God, meaning a strong sense or prompting that may not necessarily be the clear, audible voice that most people seek. On one extreme, you have God speaking to Moses through a burning bush, and on the other you have Peter literally standing right in front of Jesus as He calls him out to walk on water. Clearly God uses a variety of methods to communicate.

His methods of speaking are important, but the real value is found in responding. If we responded to even a third of what we could, our lives would be exponentially more explosive. His timing won't be convenient and most likely will interrupt the rhythms of the life you've established. Until you do something about that nudge, you won't be at peace.

His promises are intrinsically tied to our purpose. We must turn and embrace it, otherwise life will feel like a perpetual Groundhog Day. Are you ready? There are needs on this earth that God has specifically orchestrated the uniqueness of your DNA to uncover and resolve. The world is eagerly waiting for you to show up.

> There are needs on this earth that God has specifically orchestrated the uniqueness of your DNA to uncover and resolve.

It's okay to ask questions. In fact, it's quite natural. "Was that really God? How will such-and-such happen? I don't have the resources or know-how to make this happen!" Asking questions is how we get answers. That's why it's called faith—a belief that the evidence will be revealed as we engage our pursuit of His promises.

So we set out to inform ourselves to determine our next steps. And then we have another wave of a thousand thoughts: "That's for someone else! God knows my past! I don't have the character to last!" Having faith is to and persist and resist the doubts that are certain to visit. Faith requires us to consider the cost and then put a downpayment on our destiny.

Moses's original desire was to see His people set free from bondage but spending years of his life on the backside of the desert, left his hope dehydrated. He settled into a seemingly satisfying existence. He had the wife, the kids, and the land to work. But did he have peace? He had everything that the world will tell us we need in order to be satisfied.

And then the burning bush reflected the simmering and unsettling fire that could never be quenched inside him. It burnt away the frail existence of the white picket fence. The photoshopped, touch-upped image was revealed for what it really was—a form of godliness denying the fullness of the desires with him.

As this all melted away, Moses's internal fire was stirred up and he realized he could no longer live without the one thing that mattered: helping to deliver his people from the terrors of Pharoah. The fire finally burnt away the façade of his 'happy' existence, readying him to uproot his green patch of grass and head back into the desert to face… himself.

You see, before he could confront Pharoah, he needed to confront the man in the mirror.

Look around. Is there a bush on fire in your life? There is, and it's within you. It won't allow for peace until you, like Jacob, set aside everything and begin to wrestle and struggle with God for it (Genesis 32).

But the busyness of life is desperately trying to weigh you down with logistical family obligations. After all, little Johnny has to get to baseball practice somehow. Or it could be work- related, with someone needing to ensure a project is completed on time. These obviously aren't poor pursuits, but despite them we need to determine if daily life is drowning out God's voice and the snuffing out the fire within you.

One of the most common prayer requests I receive is for clarity about a person's calling and for direction for their destiny. But when you receive the guidance you seek, what will you do next? The price tag and impact on your time and effort could scare others off, but what about you? Will you keep holding on to His promises even when your progress appears to be arrested? There will be an impact on your family life, career, and social endeavors. The question is not whether God will show you His plans for your life; rather, when He does, what price will you be willing to pay for it? It will cost you something, but the eternal rewards will always outweigh your sacrifice.

Faith extends beyond simply identifying your desires and writing them down on a wish list, then calling it a goal. Calling it a goal doesn't make it a goal. Goals include putting in place a POA (plan of arrival) with a realistic view of the financial cost and impact on your time. How committed you are will determine whether you fulfill His promises and your purposes. That commitment will be evident on your calendar and in your bank statement.

Are you *gaining* full value for your effort? That's not the right question. The question is, are you *giving* a full effort according to the size and grandeur of the dreams and desires God has deposited in your DNA? At the end of the day, you get what you pay for. There are no discounts in eternity, so determine the cost and set out to pay full price!

> There are no discounts in eternity, so determine the cost and set out to pay full price!

Moses knew that the path to fulfill his faith would pass straight through Pharoah's rock- hard heart, so he consistently pounded away at that rock. He appeared before Pharoah time after time, because he knew that repeatedly presenting himself before Pharoah, plague after plague, increased both the odds of him landing in a coffin *and* securing freedom for his people. So he kept going before Pharoah.

How many times should you go back to face your opposition? Until you receive the outcomes and the breakthroughs you seek. But will you? That's up to you. What will last longer, your persistent faith or the forces opposing you? Ultimately, whatever or whoever lasts longer will always win.

> Now faith is the substance [realization] of things hoped
> for, the evidence [confidence] of things not seen.
>
> (Hebrews 11:1, NKJV)

Hebrews 11 is considered the Hall of Fame of faith, packed with ordinary people who became extraordinary by reaching for more than they could accomplish on their own. From Noah and Abraham to Rahab and David, they all believed they would experience and live in the very thing they were living for.

Their conviction, and more so their actions, suggested that a cause worth living for was also one worth dying for. Their faith was commended due to their perseverance in pursuing their promise until they possessed it. They deemed persecution, isolation, and even humiliation worth it.

Have you reached that point yet? By faith, these heroes of the faith pushed beyond their past, not allowing it to impact their future. By faith, in the absence of physical evidence, they allowed their assurance and God's approval to anchor their actions and considered their outcomes as a matter of fact—and a matter of time.

Who walks around a towering stone wall in anticipation that it will spontaneously collapse? Who extends a rod over waters waiting for them to move to the left and right? Who believes that all Jesus needs to do is say the word and even death must bow?

What about you? Are your actions anchored in the assurance that God is a rewarder of those who diligently seek Him? What waters are God calling you to step out onto? What promises are barricaded behind walls just waiting for you to step out and march around until those walls come down?

The heroes in Hebrews 11 overcame the facts of adversity, racism, and devastation to fulfill their faith through actions that glorified God. We show God our faith by pushing past the problems that plague us.

So how will you fulfill your faith? Will you wrestle with doubt or actually step out? This is the difference between boat-dwellers and water-walkers. It's the difference between those who consider doors as keeping us out versus those who think of them as ways in. Faith says that we would rather fall on our faces than sit on our hands because we would rather mess up than miss out. The difference is huge and can make all the difference in eternity.

Who is waiting on the other side of your faith to be set free? There's only one way to know. You'll have to step out in faith to make these discoveries and uncover the answers you seek.

> Now when Moses held up his hand, Israel prevailed, and when he lowered his hand [due to fatigue], Amalek prevailed.
>
> (Exodus 17:11)

Imagine what was going through Moses's mind in Exodus 17 as he saw the battle go in his favor when he kept his arms up; but when he grew tired, the Amalekites began to win again. Moses had to last longer than the lactic acid build-up in his arms and shoulders zapping his strength.

Joshua and the others learned that the strength of Moses's faith was not going to be enough. His endurance and perseverance were the keys to seeing Israel through. Perseverance can be defined as the moment when determination rises as motivation and strength fall. The persistence of your calling is evidenced by your continuous pursuit of purpose, even when you see no progress.

Faith can be viewed in terms of muscular power, which is momentary and allows for a maximum lift. But also consider the cardiovascular strength you need in order to endure through a long grind, like when you're on a treadmill, seemingly getting nowhere. Is one aspect more important than the other? The point is that it takes acts of bravery to die for something, but a whole lot more courage to live daily for your cause. The endurance of your faith will prepare you for those monumental moments when you can move from promise to possession. Faith is about enduring until the evidence comes.

The Israelites must have been exhausted marching around Jericho, both physically and mentally. Imagine how many opportunities to doubt would have had to creep in while they walked silently in circles days on end. But Joshua chose faith over fatigue! They kept keeping on until the scoreboard reflected their faith. Until those walls came down, they stayed steadfast in obedience, believing God would follow through. Keep marching until you see your victory. The heavens are waiting to be unleashed to do what they do best: blow up barricades and wipe out walls that stand between you and the fullness of your purpose. Following through is the difference between possessing a promise and obsessing over a dream. Again, your belief will be tested before fruit is manifested.

I still have a vivid memory of sitting on the toilet as a toddler when suddenly, one of my dad's pet pigeons flew in through the window. I did what any three- or four-year-old would do. I screamed at the top of my lungs!

The door was locked, but my dad pressed up against it so that I would hear his calming voice above my shrieking. "Trust me, son, it won't hurt you. Just finish up."

A few years later, I was standing on top of the front hood of my dad's Chrysler Fifth Avenue while he stood on the ground next to me. "Trust me, son, I'll catch you. Just jump."

In my early twenties, as I contemplated whether to marry my current bride of twenty-plus years, he spoke to me again. "Trust me, son, she is a woman of character. Don't mess this up!"

In every circumstance, my dad's voice didn't tell me not to worry; he told me to trust him.

Exercising our faith is represented through our trust in our heavenly Father. But it becomes difficult to trust when we feel threatened and fearful about potential failure and shame. The challenge with trust is the requirement to relinquish control. But trust isn't about losing control over your outcomes but rather building relational equity with God, and that relational equity is worth far more than the outcome we're trying to dictate in the first place.

Faith is represented in the three Hebrews boys who said, "Our God can. But even if He doesn't, we'll still trust Him to deliver the right outcome" (Daniel 3:16–18). The ultimate marker of Shadrach, Meshack, and Abednego's faith was in their willingness to place their trust in God. And when they stood up, the enemy had to stand down.

Peter faced the ridicule of his peers as he stepped out of that boat, but he had a choice to either remain small or step into his destiny. His trust triumphed over his fear of failure.

Elijah had to trust that a faithful God would follow through and send down fire.

Gideon had to trust that his tiny army of three hundred would defeat tens of thousands.

By faith, Noah built the first ever cruise ship—complete with a floating zoo! He had never experienced rain before, but he trusted God's calling and will for his life. He went all-in, so God went all-out for Noah.

By faith, Abel offered his better sacrifice without really knowing whether the God of heaven would honor and recognize it.

It will be more than uncomfortable as you step out to walk on water when all your peers are watching, waiting to see you sink. But will your trust in your heavenly Father to win the day? These heroes of faith didn't waste their time imagining what could happen. Instead, they partnered with God to make their purpose prosper. They all trusted that God would follow through on their acts of obedience. We work out our purposes without guaranteed outcomes—not because it ends well, but because we trust that His version will be worthwhile.

The fact is that the young boy David would have to face a grown, battle-tested warrior who probably consumed meals as big as David himself. The facts declared that there was zero chance of his success, but he acted in faith anyway, not the facts. His faith tilted the facts in his favor. So, who was really the underdog? Was it David or Goliath? The reality is that Goliath's size couldn't measure up to the size of David's faith.

The reality is that the stench of Lazarus's corpse was putrid after four days in the tomb, but God had another plan. Jesus showed up on the scene, and even the fact of death melted away when Jesus spoke: *Lazarus, come out!* (John 11:43)

Martin Luther King could have been assassinated in the first month, or even the first day, of his passionate pursuit of equality, but he chose not to be limited by fear. His actions were dictated by seeing himself standing upon mountaintops by faith, not threatened by sharp dogs' teeth, water cannons, or bullets.

These men defied the facts, and their faith was fulfilled when they followed through.

But again, what about you? What dictates your actions? Is it the facts of faith? These giants leveraged faith to tilt the facts in their favor. David must have seen Goliath as an ant in the presence of his God, and Jesus minimized Lazarus's tombstone as a mere inconvenience to His incredible mission.

I've always coached others to understand that it's easy to take your shots when life is going well. But you'll discover what you really believe about yourself, and what you believe about God, when you miss shots and life gets difficult. My faith was tested when my father-in-law passed away. He was a gentle soul who avoided confrontation at all costs. For almost twenty-five years, my wife and I prayed daily that he would come to experience the saving grace of the cross. Sadly, when he died, we weren't certain that such a moment ever took place.

Almost twenty-five years! Did we have faith? Certainly. Did we believe? Yes. And did we follow through? Yes.

We have learned that trusting God doesn't mean overriding His will with our wants. We have learned to live with the makes and the misses. Although that season of eternal loss was difficult, we keep taking our shots because the final buzzer hasn't gone off.

My prayer is that you won't avoid the confrontation in your own soul. My prayer is that even if you missed your shot, you will rebound well—because your God will provide another opportunity. Keep shooting your shots. It is going to happen for you, and it will be glorious!

Closing

As with Lazarus, Jesus is still calling us to come out of dead and dormant spaces. He's still resurrecting our dreams and desires, bringing them back to life!

If you feel a tug on your heart to explore more of what's in your core, chase it down and keep moving in the direction of your destiny. Your pursuit of God might not look perfect but remember to keep pressing forward. Why? Because hesitation leads to the assassination of motivation. Even when you don't feel worthy, God's grace is ready to wrap its arms around you.

If you want to chat through any of the content you have read, I will personally respond (Connect@CHBHN.net).

Cheering you on always,

Shiraz Siddique.

About CBHN

Congratulations and thank you sincerely for taking this journey towards your successful Judgment Day. The fullness of God's best life for you is in the follow through of your faith as you passionately pursue your purpose.

At times, that effort can leave us low on faith and low on fuel, and that's why the Christian Business Harvest Network exists. CBHN is the catalyst that keeps our hearts and minds moving through darker days when no one sees us or seems to care.

Consider this your invitation to join a community of like-minded believers who are striving to keep their focus strong to cross more finish lines. Email connect@CBHN.net to find out how you can benefit from this fertile soil that is multiplying seeds of finances, time, and effort in the lives of so many.

Upcoming Book:
Safe But Not Satisfied

Moses's life was filled with all the comforts the world tells us we need in order to be satisfied: family, income, and control. But a burning bush sparked his dehydrated dream to see His people free from bondage. The burning bush reflected the simmering and unsettling fire that he could no longer ignore.

Safe But Not Satisfied was written to address the uncomfortable gnawing that keeps you feeling unsettled until you turn and face it. It's not about a lack of gratefulness for what you have, but rather maximizing your full potential in God.

If your desire is to step into your future, free from the constraints of the past, then *Safe But Not Satisfied* is for you. Are you ready to explore more of what's in your core and make it a reality? You could be the person God has been incubating to be a solution to the challenges your community and the world is facing. Are you ready?

About the Author

Shiraz blends the best of his corporate and pastoral experience to help so many people fuel a passionate pursuit of their purpose. His core desire is to see more Christians break out of neutral, lukewarm living so they can reach the finish lines God has laid out for them.

As an media host, author, ministry leader, and serial entrepreneur, his motivating and inspirational style has made him a sought-after guest speaker for ministry and business events. Shiraz received his Masters in Theological Studies from Tyndale University and Seminary, strengthening his resolve to guide people in the direction of their God-given destiny.

Surrounded by a committed core team, Shiraz was instrumental in launching CBHN, the Christian Business Harvest Network, to continue the work of building up the competence and confidence of everyone he connects with.

To book a speaking engagement or a Zoom chat with Shiraz, email connect@CBHN.net.

Made in the USA
Monee, IL
07 July 2026

56551662R00089